ie Return D

Every bird has its decoy, and every man is led and misled in a way peculiar to himself....The creature that lives with a false life is soon destroyed.

— *GOETHE*

BOURGEOIS SOCIALISM

Its Rise and Collapse in America

By
Arnold Petersen

1963
NEW YORK LABOR NEWS COMPANY
61 Cliff St., New York, N.Y. 10038

It seems that there are people who by the word "revolution" understand a social wreck, a splitting off from the past absolutely. I do not so understand revolution. Revolution is simply the culminating point of evolution; and this revolution that we are about to make in our generation is intimately connected with the revolution that the so-called revolutionary fathers accomplished. To say that they were absolutely bourgeois, without any feeling for anybody else, to say that their purpose was to oppress and that that motto of Franklin [that property was the creature of society, to which society is entitled whenever society needs it] meant that, is absolutely to ignore the fact, to ignore the philosophy of history. The revolutionary fathers were oncoming capitalists, they were bourgeois, but ....they imagined that if you would allow a person free access to the opportunities of labor [that is, to property] his freedom would be guaranteed.

—DANIEL DE LEON.

(Printed in the United States of America)

Contents

5

Introduction

This sketch of "bourgeois Socialism" in America is necessarily incomplete. Volumes could be written on the subject. The author has merely attempted to sketch the background, suggest the causes and circumstances that made the phenomenon of American "bourgeois Socialism" logical and perhaps inevitable, and highlight the main events and personalities and the course they inescapably took, carrying the story to the climax so prophetically foretold by Daniel De Leon— the unavoidable decline and collapse of the "Socialist party."

When the N.E.C. of the "Socialist party," early in 1950, took steps formally to liquidate the party, there seemed little reason to doubt that the action proposed by the N.E.C. would be carried through to its logical conclusion. The S.P. was in fact dead—why not officially and at long last certify to the patent fact? Logic on the part of a Norman Thomas is hardly to be expected, but, in supporting his party's N.E.C. in its move to rid the political scene of the rotting carcass of the bourgeois S.P., he had, for once, logic and realism on his side.

However, it would appear that there survives in the S.P. an element sufficiently vocal, sufficiently effective, to have caused the illogical, the irrational, to happen. Once again lawyers and other professionals appeared on the scene, and succeeded in defeating the

Thomas liquidation proposal. Meeting in convention in Detroit, beginning on June 2, 1950, the scattered remnants of the bourgeois Socialist party voted to reject Mr. Thomas's proposal, a rejection which was equivalent to a repudiation of the six-times Presidential candidate of the reform outfit. Led by Lawyer Darlington Hoopes of Pennsylvania, the die-hards decided to maintain the fiction of a "Socialist party" a while longer. It would be idle to speculate on the precise reason for their persisting in the mummery, but one may reasonably assume that the petty material interests of some of the lawyers and politicians were the determining factors, although sentiment (especially among some of the "old-timers") undoubtedly played its part.

From the remarks of Mr. Thomas it is clear that he took his defeat with poor grace. Darlington Hoopes continues as "national chairman," and will probably emerge as the new "leader" despite the rather faint public eulogy bestowed on the retiring "leader." How long Thomas will remain in the party is anybody's guess. It seems obvious that the S.P. as such (or what is left of it) had become a millstone around his neck. And without Thomas the bogus Socialist party will have nothing with which to attract attention and secure publicity. Those who took the Socialist claims and pretensions of the S.P. at face value must view with dismay the prospect of the further decay of this dead or dying caricature of Socialism. It may be that the ghost of the corrupt party will flit across the political stage indefinitely, but it seems far more likely that another year or two will witness the final interment of the corpse—for sanitary reasons, if for no other!

Karl Marx, in a brilliant passage in his "Eighteenth Brumaire of Louis Bonaparte," sums up the folly and criminality of the "bourgeois Socialists" in attempting to revolutionize (rather, to reform) society behind its back. What Marx said nearly a hundred years ago on this head might have been written for the fatuous reformers of today who have learned nothing from history, and to whom Marxian science remains a closed book. Marx's words of warning will bear repeating here:

"It [the misled proletariat] partly throws itself upon doctrinaire experiments, 'cooperative banking' and 'labor exchange' schemes; in other words, it goes into movements in which it gives up the task of revolutionizing the old [capitalist] world with its own large collective weapons and, on the contrary, seeks to bring about its emancipation, *behind the back of society,* in private ways, within the narrow bounds of its own class conditions and, consequently, inevitably fails."

It was the pursuit of such "doctrinaire experiments" (to which might be added colonizing schemes a la the earlier Debs) that fatedly brought the S.P. to ruin and the miseducated S.P. members to despair and disillusionment. The central theme of the S.P. political fakers was that you must "sugar-coat" the "Socialist" pill—that "Socialism" must be watered down and administered in small doses. "You cannot catch flies with vinegar," they observed brightly, which called forth De Leon's terse rejoinder that Socialism is not in the business of catching flies, but of winning rational men! It was claimed by the S.P. "intellectuals" that by espousing popular, though false, measures (or measures of no concern to the workers) it would be possible to increase the number of "Socialist" followers, and in this way inject real Socialist principles into the said followers.

Obviously the theory and the practice are false. If the movement grows numerically by such methods, nothing is achieved except the enlarging of the movement's capacity for disseminating false theories and ideas. And, having taken one step in the wrong direction, the dissembler will soon find himself compelled by the logic of events to take another and yet another such step, until he finds himself entirely and indistinguishably in the very camp that opposes the program and principles presumed to be his real concern. Moreover, his followers will expect him to make good, and if he fails them (as inevitably he must) they will quickly desert him, leaving him without any following in the end. Deviousness and double-dealing ever defeat their own purpose.

But worse than that happens. The failure of the dissembler will not be attributed to his inability to make good in an otherwise supposedly sound cause. The failure will be blamed on the professed Socialist principles and program in whose name the nostrums were presented. Hence the result will be either the boosting of the numerical strength of the capitalist camp (for which the dissembler thus actually served as a recruiting agent) or the destruction of the very movement whose interests it was sought to advance by the employment of deception and fake schemes. And the dissembler will stand thoroughly discredited, trusted neither by friends nor foes.

No, society cannot be revolutionized behind its back, nor can a revolutionary class be won to the cause of Socialism by feeding it anti-Socialist ideas—self-evidently not.

Compromises break under their own weight. Compromises in the revolutionary cause result in the consolidation of the reactionary forces and the disintegration of the revolutionary forces, and fatedly so. The truth of these contentions has been demonstrated again and again in the past, and especially in the case of the bourgeois S.P. Eugene Debs, in one of his more lucid moments, warned his associates (Berger, Hillquit, *et al.*) that their policy of truckling to craft unions and the labor fakers resulted, not in socialistizing the craft unions, but in craft-unionizing the S.P.!

In simple logic there never could have been any doubt as to the ultimate fate of the miscalled Socialist party. As Marx observed in a letter to Frederick Engels (1865):

"The logic of events will speak. But the honor of the workers' party demands that it should reject fancy pictures of this kind [reforms] even before their hollowness is exposed by experience. THE WORKING CLASS IS REVOLUTIONARY OR IT IS NOTHING."

ARNOLD PETERSEN.

June 6, 1950.

Ah, you little understand this movement! The more is done for it, the more it demands. Indeed, it gauges its expectations by past works. The having rendered good services to it is looked upon by it simply as an earnest of further services to be rendered, and which it imperiously demands. It has been so with all such movements. And it is right that it is so. Nothing done is more than a duty performed.

*

It is this way. The moment a man goes crook he becomes consumed with a vitriolic hatred for the S.L.P. 'Tis natural.

*

Would you have us scourge a sin with tender omission of the sinner?

—DANIEL DE LEON.

Part One

Bourgeois Socialism

Its Rise and Collapse
in America

By Arnold Petersen

"SOMEBODY STOLE MY PLATFORM!"

—

"Somebody stole my platform!"

(St. Louis "Post-Dispatch," Aug. 29, 1933)

1

Marx and Engels On "Bourgeois Socialism"

The more a ruling class is able to assimilate the most prominent men of a ruled class, the more solid and dangerous is its rule.—MARX.

The designation "bourgeois Socialism" may sound like a contradiction in terms, since "bourgeois" and "Socialism" mutually exclude each other. However, it has justification on the same grounds that we justify the designation "utopian Socialism." A "Socialism" that is utopian is obviously no more a real Socialism than is a "Socialism" that is bourgeois. Moreover, "bourgeois Socialism," as a designation, has historic sanction. Marx and Engels used the term repeatedly in "The Communist Manifesto," and Engels did so in his excellent monograph, "The Housing Question." In "The Communist Manifesto," under the chapter heading "Conservative or Bourgeois Socialism," the authors stated:

"A part of the bourgeoisie is desirous of redressing social grievances, *in order to secure the continued existence of bourgeois society....* [The bourgeois Socialists] want all the advantages of modern social conditions without the struggles and dangers necessarily resulting therefrom. They desire the existing state of society minus its revolutionary and disintegrating elements. *They wish for a bourgeoisie without a proletariat....*" (Our italics.)

Marx and Engels continued:

"A second and more practical, but less systematic, form of this Socialism sought to depreciate every revolutionary movement in the eyes of the working class, by showing that no mere political reform but a change in the material conditions of existence in economical relations could be of any advantage to them. By changes in the material conditions of existence this form of Socialism, however, by no means understands abolition of the bourgeois [capitalist] relations of production—an abolition that can be effected only by a revolution—*but administrative reforms, based on the continued existence of these relations;* reforms, therefore, that in no respect affect the relations between capital and labor, *but, at the best, lessen the cost and simplify the administrative work of bourgeois government.*" (Our italics.)

Coming a little closer to the modern explanation of the phenomenon, "bourgeois Socialism," Frederick Engels, in "The Housing Question," observed:

"Petty-bourgeois Socialism is strongly represented in Germany down to this very hour; on the one hand by professorial Socialists and philanthropists of all sorts with whom the wish to turn the workers into owners of their dwellings still plays a great role....; and on the other hand, in the Social Democratic party itself, and even in the ranks of the Reichstag fraction, a certain petty-bourgeois Socialism finds a voice. This takes the form that while the fundamental views of modern Socialism and the demand for the transformation of all the means of production into social property are recognized as justified, however, the realization of this is declared possible only in the distant future, a future which for all practical purposes is quite out of sight."

How very familiar and modern this sounds! As a description of the conceptions and tactics of the reform Socialist party in this country (and of the Stalinist robots, too, for that matter), it is well-nigh perfect. One need only peruse the recent or current platforms of that party (or of the Communist party), or glance through the articles written by its leading lights (and by the *fuehrers* of the Stalinist outfit), to realize how uncannily close Engels came to describing in detail the weird and reactionary proposals of the S.P.—past and present, successors and kindred!

For the so-called Socialist party of America (or what is left of it) may be called the perfect example of "bourgeois Socialism," even bearing in mind the Social Democratic parties of Europe. The European parties that served as models for the S.P. in almost every detail had at least some justification for their programs of bourgeois reformism. The S.P. had none— that is, none in Socialist principle.

In Europe large chunks of feudal privileges and practices had survived and persisted throughout the nineteenth and well into the twentieth century, and feudal customs and habits of thought lingered on and in part are still encountered. It was otherwise in the United States, which never had a feudal system. The feudal trappings present were lopped off by the American Revolution that launched capitalism here in a free and unobstructed field.

How, then, account for the phenomenon in this country of a party of "bourgeois Socialism" which, though never really successful in an electoral sense, nevertheless enjoyed a period of material success far beyond that warranted by the logic of the situation? The answer, I think, is simple enough, though it is not easily given in simple terms.

2

Early Movements
Of Petty
Capitalist Reform

Many factors combined to make possible, and perhaps even inevitable, the rise of such a party of bourgeois reformism as the S.P. Fundamentally, the S.P. fulfilled certain needs of the fast maturing plutocracy; incidentally, it reflected, or attempted to reflect, the interests of the petty capitalists and the so-called intellectuals or professional groups; finally, it served as a buffer, or a shield, for the craft unions in this country. And there was nothing contradictory in this triple role, however seemingly contradictory the situation that cast the party in it.

To understand this fully, several important facts must be noted. The plutocracy, following the Civil War, had grown enormously in power and arrogance with the tremendous development of capitalism that had taken place. The two parties of capitalism, the Republican and Democratic parties, had at the turn of the century emerged as practically one party—nationally, at least. The differences between them were minor and unimportant, and even these differences were chiefly of sectional or purely local significance. The fact of the essential oneness of the two major parties was attested (among other things) by the appearance of relatively small opposition parties, heralded by such political groups as the Granger, the Greenback and the Populist movements, representing farmers, small businessmen and assortments of professional groups. All of these groups found themselves beset by the growing power and oppressive practices of corporate interests that had secured and largely maintained control of the two dominant parties. Speaking particularly of the Populist party (but with equal application to all similar groups), De Leon observed:

"The Populist party sprang from middle class motives. The middle class [the petty capitalists] believes in exploitation of labor; but exploitation of labor implies trusts and monopolies at the other end. In other words, the middle class believes in exploiting those poorer, but resents being exploited by those richer, than itself."

These rebelling petty-bourgeois groups generally designated themselves as anti-monopolist. There were the Anti-Monopoly party of Minnesota, the Anti-Monopoly party in Iowa (also referred to as the Farmers' and Laboring Men's party), the Wisconsin Reform party, the Illinois Independent Reform party, and similarly designated groups in other states. Though these groups made a lot of noise, some of them scoring local successes, and a few sending their men to Congress, they were as a whole impotent and proved themselves incapable of coping with the ruthless power of corporate interests. Later came the Henry George movement, the United Labor party, the Nationalist movement, etc., and finally the SocialistIC Labor Party. All but the last mentioned eventually succumbed in the contest. Indeed, one might say that they all succumbed, for the successor of the SocialistIC Labor Party, that is, the Socialist Labor Party, organized in 1890, was (or soon became) in all essential respects the direct opposite of its precursor.

To sum up: the rebellious and "radical middle class" elements found themselves adrift. They (or many of them) were looking for a "home." They found it—or thought they did—in the S.L.P. of the early 'nineties. Eventually they found it in the S.P. Let us see how.

Although the founding of the Socialist Labor Party in 1890, largely through the efforts and under the inspiration of the Marxist scholar, Daniel De Leon, marked a new departure and a sharp break with the old reform strivings, the break was not entirely clean. Its platform was still filled with reform planks and immediate demands, and the Party itself was far from homogeneous in point of membership. Moreover, it was largely dominated by a German element (*"die alte Genossen,"* as De Leon dubbed them) that followed the leadership of the corrupt *New Yorker Volkszeitung,* a typical *"geschaeft-blaettchen"* (business sheet), as Engels designated it. This German element carried with them from Germany the petty-chauvinistic spirit so characteristic of most immigrants from the old country. They were persistent in their endeavors to mold the American movement in the pattern of the movement of the "Fatherland," chiefly in line with Lassallean dogmas. However, De Leon soon hit his stride, and before long the S.L.P. found itself divided into two main hostile factions—the Marxist wing headed by De Leon, Henry Kuhn, Sanial and others; and the reform and craft union element led by Abraham Cahan of the Jewish *Forward,* Morris Hillquit, the ambitious and client-hungry lawyer, the *Volkszeitung* crowd, and others of their ilk.

Eventually the split took place (in 1899), as was inevitable in the circumstances. The question is not: Why did the Party split? but: Why and how did these heterogeneous and anti-Marxist elements find themselves at all in a party dedicated to Marxian Socialism? The reason has already been hinted at, and this brings us to the second part of the explanation for the performance of the S.P. as a party of "bourgeois Socialism," and as a buffer party for entrenched corporate interests.

3

Reformist Element
In the S. L. P.

The disappearance of the "anti-monopoly" parties, accordingly, did not mean the ending of the struggle of the petty bourgeoisie against plutocratic corporate power. Far from it. For one thing, within the two dominant capitalist parties—notably the Democratic party—there developed groups representing the hard pressed petty capitalists—the "middle class" elements, as they were then called. (The term "middle class" was technically wrong, because these elements in reality constituted the lower ranks of the capitalist class. However much they were at war with the plutocracy, basically their interests coincided with those of the top capitalists, inasmuch as both believed in, and strove to preserve, the capitalist system, and both had common economic interests in direct opposition to those of the workers.)

These "middle class" elements, however, soon discovered that they could not effectively serve their petty economic interests within the two old parties, however much they tried. The Bryan rebellion of the 'nineties was the last serious effort made to "capture" one of the two major parties, and, as we know, it failed utterly, though Bryan himself eventually emerged as a fairly successful, though chastened, Democratic party politician.

But only a relatively small number of the petty bourgeois derelicts "bored from within" the old parties.

As stated above, many of them were drawn to the S.L.P. of the early 'nineties, partly because the Party had not yet cut the navel string of "immediate demands" tying it to capitalism (to use De Leon's phrase), and partly because the S.L.P. was growing, commanding greater and greater attention, and acquiring an ever stronger influence, and this largely because of De Leon's dynamic presence and ever more vigorous presentation of the Socialist program.

In short, the S.L.P. was fast becoming a real menace to capitalism. For it is one thing to be subjected to the annoyance of petty groups that at worst could be only a piece of gravel in the shoe of the plutocracy, or to the annoyance of individuals who merely attacked or sought to curb particular plutocratic interests, for the rest leaving the system itself untouched. It is something quite different to have the system itself challenged, and attempts made to overthrow it together with the capitalist class.

The capitalist class, accordingly, manifested increasing concern over this potential threat to the security of its continued existence. This concern found expression in the mounting violence and viciousness of the attacks of capitalist spokesmen (outspoken or veiled) on the S.L.P., and particularly on De Leon.

They were aided in these attacks by the servile and reactionary labor leaders, or labor fakers, as De Leon dubbed them, who in turn were seconded by the petty "bourgeois Socialist" elements in the Party. One of the chief targets of De Leon's counterattacks was precisely these pro-capitalist craft unions, and particularly their chief representative, the vulgar, and essentially illiterate, "plebs leader," Samuel Gompers.

De Leon had Gompers and all his lieutenants constantly on the run, and from the plutocratic viewpoint it was seriously becoming a question of how long Gompers and his reactionary unions could survive the attacks. Capitalist interests require the existence of conservative unionism, not because capitalists love unionism per se, but because their instinct tells them that the alternative to capitalist-inspired unions and capitalist-minded union leaders is revolutionary Socialist unions and Marxian spokesmen of such unions. With the emergence of the latter, in ever increasing numbers and with ever growing understanding of the true nature of capitalism, the lot of the capitalists would not be a happy one—the fact might, indeed soon *would,* spell the doom of their robber system.

In the light of all this, it is not farfetched, then, to conclude that active agents of capitalist class interests were purposely sent into the Socialist Labor Party to join forces with those petty-bourgeois elements who grasped at the S.L.P. of the 'nineties as a drowning person grasps at a straw; to join forces, moreover, with the pro-capitalist union apologists and the adventurers and self-seekers who ever flock into "unorthodox" movements, having failed of material success in the general capitalist world.

However this may be, the cleavage in the S.L.P. became sharper and ever more distinct—the revolutionary element (the Marxists) on the one side, the reform, anti- or pseudo-Marxist element on the other side. And although many questions divided the two sides—such questions as reform or revolution, the tax question, immigration policy, party ownership of the press, state and local autonomy, party discipline, etc., etc.—the dominant, the burning, overriding question was the nature, form, proper functioning and true principles of working class unionism. As De Leon put it, "These principles of practice turned upon unionism." And he added: "This fact must be distinctly kept in mind. It explains all subsequent developments."

And all subsequent developments have confirmed De Leon's prognosis and sustained his prescience.

In a magnificent summary entitled "The Socialist Movement in America," De Leon has sketched the circumstances and the causes that led to the formation of the S.L.P. and the S.P., and the inevitableness of the course each pursued. This was published in the *Daily People* forty-one years ago, having been written originally for the 1908 Almanac of the then Hungarian S.L.P. organ, *Nepakarat*. This brilliant article fits in perfectly with the theme of this address, and I can do no better than to include it here.

4

De Leon's Sketch
Of the American Movement

"History [wrote De Leon] cannot be written until there is an ample supply of material therefor. As history is not mere chronology, and is essentially descriptive, the present status of a movement cannot be properly described before there is at hand a sufficiency of consecutive data to enable the historian, with some degree of certainty, to gauge the trend of events. It may seem paradoxical, yet it is true, that real history must not be 'retrospective' only, it must be 'prospective' also. While the past tells us whence we come, the present, and the future developments that the present points to, are material in understanding the past. Upon these general principles the history of the Socialist movement in America is hardly yet to be written. The present is still in too chaotic a state to justify accurate conclusions upon the past, much less to justify an accurate forecast. Under present circumstances, 'Histories of American Socialism' [by such shoddy intellects, for example, as Hillquit, Simons, Oneal, and others.—A.P.] are mere catchpenny undertakings. Sketches are all that the subject allows today. Such a sketch—and a very rough one at that—is all I can present to our Hungarian comrades.

"There is ever a morbid desire to rise to the very source of a movement. The endeavor to 'trace the Socialist movement of America to its source' illustrates the morbidness of that failing. It illustrates even more —it illustrates how purely dogmatic these [would-be] Marxists are who have attempted the job of 'tracing to its source,' and how skin-deep their Marxism is. Their 'tracings' sound as the talk of a geographer would sound who started to 'trace the source' of a river in the clouds. No doubt the water that river is made of comes to a large extent from clouds. But the clouds we see may never descend into that particular river; moreover, obscure underground springs may be important feeders to the stream. I shall omit the 'source hunt.' I shall limit myself in this sketch to the citing of a series of facts. Let others coordinate them and write their history.

"From a vast amount of material, Marx generalizes that the bourgeois Republic of the United States, being at the stage of its physical development, was still at the conservative stage. The classes had not yet acquired that consistency which is unacquirable so long as visions exist of material success. That was the material that Socialism had to work upon. As to such material Socialism was premature.

"The prematureness of Socialism in America was emphasized by the circumstance that those who, a generation or so ago, introduced the word 'Socialism' were not, generally, what the introducers of Socialism had been in Germany—a native intellectual injection ahead of the material conditions that would call for a movement.

"They were neither native nor, as a rule, intellectual. They were expatriated Germans whose Socialism consisted mainly in negations, and whose intelligence of the subject was so superficial that it kept them from a correct understanding of the conditions of the country of their adoption. This lack of understanding caused that element to divide into two legitimate opposites.

"One element threw Socialism wholly overboard. Its slogan was: 'Socialism is good enough in Germany, but not in America. Here everyone can grow rich. Look at me. I am only a short time here and already I have got a good business, and have my own house [mortgaged].' Or: 'Socialism is good enough in Germany, but not in America. Don't you see I don't need to serve in the Army here.'

"The other element clung to the word 'Socialism' as to a superstition. Its slogan was: 'The Americans are too hopelessly stupid and corrupt. They can never understand Socialism'—and with this slogan they consoled themselves for their misfortune in having come to '*Malheurica*,' their favorite pun upon America. This double circumstance threw an extraneous obstacle in the path of Socialism. The use of a name by such elements rendered the thing itself unpleasant.

"Simultaneously with these events economic development went on. Its sediment of experience—however crude, however imperfect or visionary—was a series of utopian outbreaks. The first was the Greenback movement in the early 'seventies; the second was the Single Tax movement; the third was the Nationalist (Bellamy) movement. It is a notable fact that each of these movements, in succession, began outside of the camp of the working class; each was captained and crewed by intellectuals of the middle and upper classes—Peter Cooper, Henry George, Edward Bellamy; each refused to recognize the working class as a separate socio-political entity; each proposed to bring salvation 'to the people'; and each went down, leaving the extinguishing candle in the hands of workingmen—the only element that stuck.

"Out of these various sediments—aided step by step by economic evolution—rose the first party of Socialism in the land, the Socialist Labor Party, in 1890.

"The appearance of the S.L.P. in 1890 was the first substantive manifestation of a Socialist movement in the United States. The Party started not merely upon abstract principles of Socialism, it started with some very concrete principles of practice. The former need no mention, they are international. The latter were more typical of American conditions. These principles of practice turned upon *unionism*. This fact must be distinctly kept in mind. It explains all subsequent developments.

"The S.L.P. of America started its existence with the question of unionism as its cornerstone. The unions in existence were 'pure and simple,' that is, they held to the principle of brotherhood between capital and labor, and 'no politics in the union.' The two principles rendered the union a corrupt body, managed by the capitalists through their labor lieutenants, the officers of the unions.

"The S.L.P. took an emphatic stand, and declared that the union could not help but be steeped in politics, hence the bona fide union was bound to be in Socialist politics. A stand like that, once taken, was bound to develop to its logical conclusions, and at the same time drop whatever errors originally clung to it.

"The development was rapid. In 1896 the S.L.P.

was mainly instrumental in setting up the Socialist Trade and Labor Alliance, an economic organization that proclaimed its intimate relations with politics and pronounced the S.L.P. its political expression. The S.T. & L.A. was no sooner launched than it became the target for the bitter assault of the A. F. of L. The struggle was, of course, carried into the Party by the representatives of the A. F. of L., and a conflict ensued that culminated in a split in 1899. One portion of the S.L.P. pulled out and declared 'neutrality' toward unionism, while the body of the S.L.P. pronounced 'neutrality' only a mask behind which to conceal partisanism in favor of corrupt unionism. The struggle, carried on up to 1899 within the S.L.P., now continued between the S.L.P. on the one side, and, on the other, a new party, in which the bolters from the S.L.P. were incorporated.

"This new party consisted of heterogeneous elements. It had sprung up in the West under the leadership of Eugene V. Debs. As far as the Western party received a character from Mr. Debs, its policy was hostile to that of the bolters from the S.L.P. Mr. Debs had risen into prominence as a founder of revolutionary unions against the reactionary brotherhoods of railroad employees. His name stood essentially for exactly the opposite of the bolters from the S.L.P., who proposed to 'bore from within' only, a slang phrase that meant 'Don't disturb the labor leaders.' Unity between the Debs element and the bolters from the S.L.P. would have been impossible but for the circumstance that the question of unionism was not considered essential by the Debs element. The point of contact between the two was the utopianism of both—the bolters from the S.L.P. held to the utopian idea that the 'union was a vanishing thing' and therefore should be humored; the Debs element held to the utopian idea that votes would be enough to overthrow capitalism. The two utopianisms merged into one. The Socialist party was formed.

"The formation of the Socialist party gave impetus to the development of the Socialist Labor Party principle. The S.L.P. principle soon took shape in the principle that the union was an essential factor in the emancipation of the working class. The Marxian motto, 'Only the union can give birth to the true party of labor,' became the guiding light of the S.L.P. The Party laid main stress upon the organization of the working class into revolutionary unions and considered the ballot, however important, useful and necessary, a secondary consideration. The S.P., on the contrary, held the union to be unimportant, the ballot everything.

"Within five years after the issue had been thus presented, the economic events of the land gave birth to a manifestation that confirmed the S.L.P. principle. The Industrial Workers of the World was organized, mainly by revolters from the A. F. of L. The S. T. & L. A. joined the new body. Experience had clarified many a division of the S.P., and they gave their adherence to the I.W.W. Immediately the scenes enacted when the S. T. & L. A. was founded began to be reenacted. The I.W.W. became the target for a fierce onslaught. A conspiracy was concocted to disrupt it and came near succeeding in 1905. The conspiracy being baffled, the Socialist movement entered upon its present stage.

"The S.P. principle of 'neutrality' is thoroughly

discredited. Every day the struggle between the two parties brings out more and more clearly that 'neutrality' means, on the one side, economic corruption and encouraging of craft union scabbery; on the other side, political corruption through the sacrifice of principle to votes.

"The S.L.P. principle that the vote is worthless and political victory calamitous if the Industrial Union is not organized and ready to take and hold the reins of government—that principle is steadily gaining ground.

"The S.P. vote is dropping heavily. Votes being all that the S.P. had, its downfall is inevitable.

"As to the S.L.P., the conflict has greatly affected its voting strength also. But because the S.L.P. had a principle that is triumphantly asserting itself, its victory is assured."

5

The Assault On Socialism

The detailed story of the split in 1899 and the circumstances attending it have been told repeatedly in the literature of the S.L.P., and need not be recounted here. The struggle that led to the split was a long and bitter one.

With the launching of the Socialist Trade and Labor Alliance in 1895, subsequently officially endorsed by the S.L.P. at its Ninth Convention in 1896, the fight was on in earnest and in the open. In the language of Marx, into this battle there were summoned "the most violent, mean and malignant passions of the human breast, the Furies of private interest."

What these "Furies of private interest" were, we know. First and foremost there was the interest of craft unionism, and the personal vested interests of the labor leaders in craft unions. For the greater part these leaders were ignorant, illiterate and utterly unprincipled. They were in their posts to serve a very special purpose, aside from securing for themselves a comfortable living and a carefree old age.

That special primary purpose was to keep the workers in line, to keep them from kicking over the traces—to see to it that capitalist interests were fully served by maintaining working class docility, by rendering the workers loyal slaves to the capitalist masters. And if or when the workers did rebel, it was the function of the fakers to keep them from going too far and to effect settlements that would leave things much as they were before. In short, the craft unions (being the "bulwarks of capitalism," as the *Wall Street Journal* put it) and the labor leaders were expected to keep the workers in ignorance of their true class interests, and, above all, they were expected to prevent the Socialists from reaching the workers with the Marxian message of working class emancipation. [1]

In this, as we know, they succeeded only too well. But they did not succeed without help. Though all labor leaders (or "labor lieutenants," as the astute pluto-

---

[1] A writer in the "International Socialist Review" (March, 1910) reported this revealing incident:

"About ten years ago Ralph M. Easley [notorious plutocratic hatchet-man] came into the private office of the late Marcus A. Hanna, in Cleveland, Ohio, and to him unfolded a plan whereby the labor organizations of the country could be controlled and made to serve a useful purpose to the big capitalists. He pointed out that the huge vanity of the labor leaders was one weak point to work upon and that, coupled with the opinions that they sometimes voiced regarding the identity of interests between the employer and his employees, could be turned to great advantage, if proper means were utilized."

"Proper means" were utilized and Mark Hanna had his "labor lieutenants" where he wanted them, at his service and at his beck and call. And praising the notorious labor faker, John Mitchell, of the United Mine Workers, as a "grand man," the canny old Scotsman, Andrew Carnegie, said, "The more I get in touch with union labor [fakers], the more I get to understand and respect it. I am going to be a better and better union man as I get better acquainted with its leading representatives."

The crafty plutocrats, Mark Hanna and Andrew Carnegie, knew the uses of the modern plebs leaders. And so do their heirs of today! The names of the labor fakers have changed, as have the names of the plutocrats, but the species in both categories have remained unchanged. And so, unhappily, have the workers in their failure to understand the true motives of their deadliest foes.

cratic politician, Mark Hanna, called his "labor boys," Gompers & Co.)—though all these labor fakers were essentially one in outlook and purpose, outwardly they fell into two groups: the utterly crude and avowedly pro-capitalist species who declaimed against the "evil of Socialism," and the craftier and more dangerous kind who professed to be Socialists and pretended belief in the possibility of turning the reactionary unions into Socialist ones, and of converting the "heathen" labor leaders into good Socialists. "Boring from within," they called it. It was this latter element that De Leon contended with inside the S.L.P. prior to the split.

This element found made-to-order allies in certain newspapers and editors who (apart from supporting pro-capitalist unionism) also had special private interests to serve. Characteristically enough, the two most important papers supporting the anti-Socialist unions were printed in foreign languages. The first was the *New Yorker Volkszeitung,* founded in 1878, and, as previously mentioned, the center of the German-nativistic, German-speaking element. Its editor was one Alexander Jonas, a shallow-minded ignoramus who had no conception of the meaning of Socialism, and who catered to all the prejudices and German-nativistic notions of the immigrants. His hatred of De Leon and the S.L.P. knew no limit, and his paper was virulent in its attack on the sound Socialist element and as emphatic in its support of Gompers unionism as De Leon and his associates were in opposing it.

Ten years after the split this corrupt paper, no longer perceiving any further need of dissembling, frankly acknowledged its part in disrupting the Social-ist movement. In its issue of September 2, 1909, it stated: "Yes, the *New Yorker Volkszeitung* went so far in its defense of the American Federation of Labor that it accepted the risk of a split in the Socialist move-ment of America in order to prevent a split in the trade union movement of the land, and to keep up the Amer-ican Federation of Labor as the united [!] body of American unionism."[2]

The phrase "accepted the risk" must be taken in a strictly Pickwickian sense, for the paper had no qualms or illusions at any time as to the purpose and conse-quences of its anti-Socialist acts. It was this same pa-per that spewed its foulest venom on De Leon when he lay dead.

From its very beginning to its unduly protracted end, the sheet was a foul blot upon the fair name of Socialism. Its primary concern was, of course, to serve the interests of its private owner—to make money, hence Frederick Engels's contemptuous reference to it as a "business sheet." And it had concluded that the way to do that was to support the corrupt A. F. of L. fakers and the other professional business interests that gathered around it.

---

[2] Max Hayes, writing in the "International Socialist Review" for May, 1905, brazenly boasted that the "bourgeois Socialist" reformers in the S.L.P. of the 'nineties succeeded in doing what the capitalist class could not do, destroy Marxian Socialism in America. Though his boast was a vain and foolish one, this does not alter the fact that they tried to do so (in capitalist interests), and that they gloried in their infamous treachery. Hayes wrote: "...The trade unionists and sympathizers [!] se-ceded from the S.L.P. and practically destroyed that party, **which is more than our Republican and Democratic brethren have ever done....**"

During the first world war it changed tactics (or seemed to do so) by denouncing the Kaiser, undoubtedly prompted by the consideration that this was the profitable thing to do. But here it was wrong, for the result was a loss in circulation and revenue from which it never recovered. Then along came the Bolshevik Revolution, and, again concluding that here was something new to be exploited, it climbed on the Russian bandwagon (under the editorship of one Ludwig Lore, formerly assistant to Alexander Jonas). But this new effort also failed utterly.

Now on its last legs the sheet took up the business of anti-Hitlerism, providing "refuge" for certain Social Democratic politicians and writers who had fled from Germany when Hitler rose to power. As if ashamed of its past record (as well it might be), its name was changed to *Neue Volkszeitung,* and, under the editorship of one of the expatriated German Social Democrats, it rounded out its career by giving open support to capitalist politicians. Its funeral oration was delivered recently by a notorious renegade, one Wm. E. Bohn, editor of the anti-Socialist sheet, *The New Leader.* Mr. Bohn, shedding copious tears, and prefacing his remarks by saying that the paper had been "proved correct in a long list of contentions during and since the war," commented in part as follows: "The *Neue Volkszeitung* [nee *New Yorker Volkszeitung*] supported most of Roosevelt's domestic policies ....," adding that it had also "supported President Truman's political campaign and legislative program." (The *New Leader,* August 27, 1949.)

This was the paper that took a leading part in the fight against De Leon's and the S.L.P.'s sound Socialist policies and propaganda. From first to last it presented itself as a perfect example of "bourgeois Socialism."

6

Abe Cahan and The "Forward"

The other paper that took up the cudgels on behalf of pro-capitalist unionism, attacking De Leon and Marxian Socialism violently and viciously, was Abraham Cahan's paper, the Jewish *Forward* (*Vorwaerts*). This paper was, if anything, an even more venal supporter of the labor fakers than the *Volkszeitung,* and at least as typical of "bourgeois Socialism" as its German confrere. Cahan was the chief owner of the sheet, and it excelled even the *Volkszeitung* as a *"geschaeft"* paper, proving a far more profitable commercial venture. It aped the methods of Hearst's corrupt journalism, and eventually grew very rich. Its treason to Socialism paid off—in wealth, that is. A grateful capitalist class and its press have bestowed recognition and honor on the sheet, and especially on its chief editor and owner, Abraham Cahan. On the occasion of the *Forward's* 50th anniversary, the New York *Times* eulogized the paper and Cahan in these terms:

"Tomorrow the Jewish *Daily Forward* reaches its half-century mark. Like its 87-year-old editor, Abraham Cahan, it is one of the finest products of the East Side, venerable now but still vigorous. Under Mr. Cahan's leadership it has steadily expanded from an almost moribund doctrinaire sheet into a great and influential newspaper."

"Moribund doctrinaire" is the *Times's* delicate way of describing Mr. Cahan's lip service to Socialism, in the 'nineties. The New York *Times* amplified its eulogy in these revealing words:

"In the *Forward* he [Cahan] found a small, dull Socialist party [sic!] organ and soon transformed it into a progressive newspaper devoted largely to Americanizing the newly arrived immigrant."

This is deserved praise bestowed on a loyal servitor of plutocratic interests by plutocracy's chief organ in America. The "Americanizing" consisted chiefly in rendering these newly arrived workers fit subjects for capitalist exploitation and easy prey for the labor fakers.

At the anniversary celebration in New York, Mr. Cahan was "honored" by outstanding capitalist representatives, including the errand boy of Ultramontanism, Mayor William O'Dwyer; the chief of capitalist labor lieutenants, William Green, and others. Congratulatory messages were received from President Truman, ex-Governor Lehman, Henry Morgenthau and others. There is an Old World saying that goes something like this: "The devil knows his own." The plutocracy recognizes in the "bourgeois Socialist" Cahan one of its very own. [3]

---

[3] During the summer of 1950 Abe Cahan attained his ninetieth birthday. It was "celebrated" on September 9, and once again the capitalist class and its spokesmen showered their praise on the man who has served them and their robber system so well. The big capitalist dailies bestowed the usual encomiums on one of their most faithful allies and obedient servitors. The ultra-plutocratc New York "Times" (September 9, 1950) led off with an editorial entitled "Fighter for Freedom"! The editorial concluded: "He [Cahan] has done much to make this a better and stronger [capitalist] America." Amen! His

One who knew Cahan and his corrupt sheet inside and out has described the character and methods of this present-day darling and organ of the plutocracy. He is Joseph Schlossberg, once a member of the Socialist Labor Party, and one-time editor of its Jewish organ; also former General Secretary of the wealthy Amalgamated Clothing Workers Union, and now a pet if not a pensioner of the Cahan coterie. Mr. Schlossberg wrote in 1910 as follows:

"The *Vorwaerts* [*Forward*] is the Yiddish yellow journal par excellence. There is nothing yellower in the Jewish language in any part of the world. It is yellow in its 'Socialist' writings. Among its 'Socialist' editorials the reader will find such 'revolutionary' instructive matters as congratulations to President [Theodore] Roosevelt upon the marriage of his daughter. In other departments the most obscene and morally disgusting points are taken out from a 'juicy' story, are magnified and illustrated, and printed under a suggestive headline. . . It has reduced its own writers to mere mechanical quill-pushers without will or individuality. Some time ago, it locked out a part of its editorial staff, and the secret then leaked out—through its own columns—that the editorial department of the *Vor-*

---

admiring friends—the treacherous labor fakers—arranged a "luncheon" in his honor, and the now familiar messages poured in from politicians, capitalists and fakers of all stripes. The congratulants included the chief of the executive committee of the capitalist class, President Truman; the labor-hating servant of the plutocracy, Governor Thomas E. Dewey; banker and Senator H. Lehman; and many others of the same ilk. Among the capitalist labor lieutenants who "honored" Cahan was the head of the Amalgamated Clothing Workers, Mr. Jacob Potofsky, successor to the man who long ago told the truth about Cahan—Joseph Schlossberg.

waerts is a literary sweatshop with a 'foreman' as slave driver at its head. On the whole the *Vorwaerts* is a tremendous engine of demoralization for the Jewish workingmen."

There is more along similar lines in Mr. Schlossberg's appraisal of this venal sheet, but what has been quoted will suffice. This, then, was the second influential paper that (in the name of Socialism!) fought the efforts of the S.L.P. and De Leon to keep the movement clean and honest and to continue the political and economic organizations on a sound Marxian basis. No wonder these corrupt sheets (and their owners and publishers) receive praise and favors from capitalist interests. From the plutocratic standpoint these "bourgeois Socialist" elements have richly earned both. What history's judgment will be need not be in doubt. Infamy and treason have a way of recording themselves in the annals of mankind, and their perpetrators invariably find their places in the rogues' gallery of history.

There were, of course, other papers and editors who pursued courses similar to those of the *Volkszeitung* and *Vorwaerts,* but an account of these would be repetitious.[4] They all had the same motivations, the

---

[4] Mention should, however, be made here of that notorious swindle sheet, the "Appeal to Reason," a "Socialist party" weekly with perhaps the largest circulation ever attained by any "bourgeois Socialist" paper in the United States. It became notorious for its promotion of stocks and bonds to enrich its private owners, whereby innocent victims were roped in to the tune of hundreds and thousands of dollars. The situation became so scandalous that a resolution was presented to the 1910 congress of the S.P. (it was defeated!) in which it was stated that "the stock gambling game in the party has increased to such an extent as to demand action by which the

personalities involved were cast in similar molds, and their "rewards" were the same, though varying in degree, and not all having the "happy ending" of the Jewish *Forward*. Most of them are now forgotten, and deservedly so. They were all alike in their hatred of De Leon, and in their mad striving for recognition by the labor fakers, and when the break came most of the editors, and all the papers except THE PEOPLE and some foreign language organs, deserted to the "bourgeois Socialist" camp—that is, to the camp of anti-Marxism, the camp of the working class enemy.

---

party may be purged of all the corruption inseparable from this most despicable of all capitalistic schemes...," and it was demanded that all papers (meaning specifically the "Appeal to Reason" and "Wilshire's Magazine") "engaged in selling stocks and bonds in mining, oil and all other speculative enterprises" be excluded from the list of recognized party organs.

Probably the most brazen offender in promoting "gold brick" schemes was "Wilshire's Magazine" (weekly), also privately owned, but listed as a party organ. Upton Sinclair, in his autobiography, wrote:

" 'The Appeal to Reason' was a gift to them from a real estate speculator with a conscience [?], old J. A. Wayland.... 'Wilshire's Magazine' was a gift from a bill-board advertising man with a sense of humor. So long as his money lasted we took his gift with thanks; if his gold mining gamble [swindle] had succeeded, we would all have made money, and had a still bigger magazine, and all would have been lovely"!

Neither publication survived the first world war—both expired in infamy. A loyal S.P. writer declared in 1928: "The 'Appeal to Reason' with its immense circulation had become pro-war under another name, 'The New Appeal' "! ("Labor and Farmer Parties in the United States, 1828-1928," by N. Fine.) And so on, **ad infinitum, ad nauseam!**

44

AN IMPORTANT ANNOUNCEMENT TO THE PUBLIC

Members of the Newspaper Guild of New York who are employes of the Jewish Forward, the Jewish Day and the Jewish Journal are being forced to call a strike at those three Jewish dailies on Tuesday, April 10, at 3:30 p. m.

The reason is simple. After several months of negotiations including sessions with the U.S. Mediation Service, the managements of those three newspapers are refusing their workers a satisfactory contract. This we say is not bargaining in good faith. The old contract expired December 31, 1950.

Employes of the Jewish Forward, Day and Journal who belong to the Newspaper Guild are in the lowest pay brackets in the respective shops. They cannot possibly get along on their present salaries.

In an effort to reach a satisfactory agreement, the Guild has shaved its wage demand to a $5 general increase. It is almost two years since employes of the three papers received a wage increase. Even the government recognizes there has been at least a 10 per cent rise in the cost of living in that period.

Thus far, the best management has offered is $2.50 plus an additional amount (for a total of about $3.12) to cover payment of the hospitalization plan. Management refused to budge from that position at a session before the U.S. Mediation Service last Tuesday, April 3. This management offer certainly is inadequate. Management's latest offer doesn't even equal five per cent.

The three Jewish dailies are big and wealthy newspapers. Our demands are minimal. The increase will not wholly meet the rising cost of living, but will help in part.

We are asking for your help in our struggle for a just and satisfactory contract. If the paper is not published, you will understand. We do not want to strike unless we are forced to do so.

Wire, write or telephone the publishers of those three newspapers and demand that they engage in true collective bargaining with their employes.

The addresses of the papers are:

Jewish Forward, 175 E. Broadway, GRamercy 5-8000.

Jewish Day, 183 E. Broadway, ORchard 4-3300.

Jewish Morning Journal, 77 Bowery, CAnal 6-7200.

Do It Today!
Thank You

Members of the Jewish Forward, Jewish Day and Jewish Journal Units
Newspaper Guild of New York
Local 3, American Newspaper Guild (CIO)

McCarthy Supplies Reports

WASHINGTON

experience—thanks to the spies—was at hand for Russia... without... he...

Abe Cahan's "Forward" still (1951) at the same labor-sweating game

(Cahan died on August 31, 1951, at the over-ripe age of 91, mourned and praised by the plutocracy he served so well)

The Labor Movement is entitled to, and needs all the knowledge of the age. Much of this knowledge cannot be the contribution of the proletariat. It has had no opportunity to gather such knowledge. Such knowledge must be the contribution of men from the upper classes who plant themselves upon the class interests of the proletariat. No sensible workingman would exclude such contributors. All sensible workingmen will invite them. The workingman who does the contrary does not do so in the interest of his class. He has some vicious scheme to nurse, and he insults his class by a posture that implies his own class is too dense to see through him.

—DANIEL DE LEON.

7

The Legal
Vultures

The third element within the early S.L.P. fighting to protect the pro-capitalist unions, and pursuing a "bourgeois Socialist" course of reform, was the so-called intellectuals. This element was made up mainly of lawyers, hired writers, nondescript authors, preachers or ex-preachers and here and there a professor or an artist. There were also some professional "social uplifters" and "do-gooders," all or most of them ignorant of Socialism, and all or most of them susceptible to the wiles of the defenders of pro-capitalist unions and allied interests.

The lawyers were the most aggressive and influential and had the greatest stake in the craft union movement. For most of them had started their legal careers by defending union members, drawing up contracts, etc., and had grown wealthy by handling such cases.

The most successful among them at that time was, or eventually became, the crafty and unscrupulous Morris Hillquit, who had come to America from Russia in 1885 at the age of 15. He worked in the tailoring trade to begin with, and with true instinct soon became a minor labor official, for some time holding office as secretary of the United Hebrew Trades of New York. His experience in this capacity may or may not have given him the idea that there was money to be made by a lawyer in handling union legal cases. Be that as it may, Mr. Hillquit took up the study of law, and eventually was admitted to the bar, hanging up his shingle at 132 Nassau Street, New York City, as Morris Hillkowitz, Attorney at Law. For a while the S.L.P. organ, THE PEOPLE, carried an advertisement (yes, we even advertised lawyers in those days!) under his original name, which he later changed to the simpler and less alien-sounding Morris Hillquit. Our future corporation lawyer and Wall Street plunger was fast becoming "Americanized"!

The New York *Evening Post* reported early in 1914 that Morris Hillquit had "plunged" in Wall Street, losing a substantial amount of money. But this was not the gentleman's only experience in Wall Street, or with corporate interests. In 1917 it was revealed that "labor lawyer" Hillquit was also attorney for the huge Burns Brothers corporation, wholesale dealers in coal and ice. It was also revealed that Mr. Hillquit was a stockholder in the Burns Brothers Coal Corporation, a company that had come in for considerable censure during the 1916 congressional election in which Hillquit was a candidate. Mr. Hillquit had denounced corporations for raising prices (the high cost of living was the "burning issue" in that campaign—and a perennial issue with reformers of all stripes), and Mr. Hillquit's corporation was charged with being one of the worst offenders in this respect.

In January of 1917 the Burns Brothers Ice Corporation was being sued, and to the corporation's attorney, Morris Hillquit, fell the task of defending it. Hillquit, however, did not appear in court in person, but sent his law partner, Alexander Levene, who, be it noted, was the secretary of the ice corporation!! The plaintiffs were represented by Fiorello La Guardia, later Mayor of New York City! The New York *Evening Journal* of January 16, 1917, gave the following account of the sordid affair:

"Morris Hillquit, defeated Socialist candidate for Congress at the recent election, was revealed in the Supreme Court today as a stockholder in the Burns Brothers Ice Corporation, one of the 'soulless entities' to which he referred in his campaign speeches as 'grinding down the poor laborers.'

"The disclosure of Hillquit's corporate connections was made by F. H. La Guardia, Congressman-elect on the Republican ticket from the Fourteenth District, in the trial before Justice Francis K. Pendleton of the suit of Frank B. and Walter W. Whitesell against the ice corporation.

"La Guardia declared that Hillquit not only holds stock in but is attorney for the ice corporation, which, he asserted, has been freezing out small independent coal and ice dealers in New York. The Burns corporation, asserted La Guardia, also worked its employees so hard that they wished to quit their jobs, but discovered that they were so tied up by agreements they could not do so.

" 'They were as helpless as slaves in the days before the Civil War,' said Attorney La Guardia.

"Hillquit did not appear in court, but his interests were looked after by his partner, Alexander Levene, who is secretary of the ice corporation."

It is clear that by 1917 "labor lawyer" and corporation attorney Hillquit had thoroughly learned the trick of working both sides of the street and both ends against the middle, ever with an eye to the main chance and the social, political and financial enhancement of Morris Hillquit, noble "humanitarian" and self-sacrificing "Socialist"!

However, let us return to the Hillquit of the earlier days.

Hillquit did not figure prominently in the struggle of the 'nineties except toward the end of it. He had, of course, been lined up with the *Volkszeitung-Forward* crowd right along, and, when he did take an active part in the disruptive assault on the Party in 1899, he came well primed and fully trained. What caused him to be chosen as the leader of the anti-Socialist and pro-craft union element is somewhat difficult to say. The man was shallow, largely self-taught, and had not yet reached the age when experience and independent reading and study often more than make up for the lack of an academic career. However, what he lacked in knowledge and experience was (for his own private purpose, and for the purposes of his co-conspirators) made up for by an unusual degree of cunning and craftiness, which, combined with unscrupulousness, ambition and extraordinary energy, made him an effective ally and eventual leader of the disrupters.

With Hillquit, as with the corrupt editors and the "socialistic" labor leaders and the rest of the "intellectuals," the motivating force that drove him on was the lust for money and public acclaim. If he could have satisfied these cravings in out-and-out capitalist circles, it is doubtful that he would ever have troubled himself about the labor or Socialist movement. But, in view of his antecedents, his lack of scholastic training, and his original lack of contacts with influential personalities in bourgeois society, it is extremely doubtful that he would ever have gone very far as a practitioner in the general field of law.

In the setting in which he found himself, and with his peculiar moral and mental make-up, he was ideally cast for the role of "labor lawyer," and as such he became the model, the classical example, for the horde of S.P. lawyers that were produced during the ensuing 25 or 30 years.

Notable among Hillquit's disciples and imitators is Louis Waldman, who has succeeded financially as well as, if not better than, Hillquit did. Waldman, a younger man, was another typical "bourgeois Socialist" with an eye to the main chance. That gentleman is now a stanch supporter of capitalism, figuring prominently in election campaigns of the old major parties, after a sojourn in American Labor party and Liberal party politics.

However, Hillquit had carved out for himself a prosperous career from the sweat and toil of the dues-paying members of the craft unions. It was reported that he charged fabulous fees for drawing up union contracts. An example of such huge fees comes to my mind. In 1916 Arthur E. Reimer was the S.L.P. presidential candidate, and in the course of his campaign he went to Paterson, N.J., to speak. On the train he met Joseph Schlossberg, then the General Secretary of the Amalgamated Clothing Workers Union and a fellow member of the S.L.P. The A.C.W. had just signed a contract that had been drawn up by Hillquit, and, as Reimer told me later, Schlossberg casually remarked to him that the union had paid Hillquit $25,000 for his services!

With such fees to be collected from pro-capitalist unions generally, it is understandable why Hillquit could not see eye to eye with De Leon and the S.L.P. as regards the exposure of, and attacks on, reactionary craft unionism. Lincoln's story about the conservative preacher who could not read the word in the Bible when a gold coin was placed over it illustrates the point. Inevitably Hillquit and his fellow exploiters of the labor movement were placed in direct opposition to Socialist principles and policies, and inescapably De Leon became a mortal foe of Hillquit's "bourgeois Socialism," through which the latter derived his substantial income. And so, when the break came in 1899, Hillquit became, as we have noted, head and front of the anti-Marxist element that had sought to oust the Marxist De Leon and his associates from positions of influence in the Socialist Labor Party.

After the split the Hillquit crowd sought, through the courts, to secure possession of S.L.P. property and its official organ. For a while they advertised themselves as the Socialist Labor Party and issued a paper that they named *The People,* otherwise known as "the bogus *People*." They lost every round in the courts, as they had previously lost their physical fight to secure possession of S.L.P. property and headquarters. Hillquit's failure in the courts might be regarded by some persons as a measure of his "learnedness" as a lawyer, but in view of the facts and the logic of the situation it is difficult to see how any lawyer could have won in a cause so palpably wrong and unrighteous.

In an editorial on the launching of the *Daily People* (July 3, 1910), De Leon refers to the conspiracy against the Party, a conspiracy that somewhat hastened the birth of the first English-language Socialist daily in America. Said De Leon:

"From the day that . . . . the launching of the *Daily People* cast its unmistakable, well-defined shadow across the path of the conspirators, the conspiracy began to assume a mass character. The visionary and reactionary hostile elements above named [the *Volkszeitung* crowd and allies] reached out for further allies. Their kindred, more pronouncedly impure even than themselves, flocked to their standard—Anarchists of both the rose and the dirty water persuasion; anti-Socialist labor lieutenants, corporals and sergeants of the capitalist class; Christian Socialist preachers without pulpits; lawyers without briefs; fishy professionals; promoters of get-rich-quick and other three-card-monte schemes against the unsuspecting working class; hungry politicians; thirsty editors and literati, etc., etc.; all rushed together, a veritable mob of barbarians, upon the S.L.P., the citadel of the Party, the *Daily People,* being instinctively the objective of all."

Verily, a latter-day barbarian assault on the Capitoline Hill!

8

Self-Analysis
By the S. P. Crowd

Following the unsuccessful attempt to usurp the name and rights of the Socialist Labor Party, the Hillquit group merged their fortunes with other groups claiming or pretending to be Socialist.

But before this "unity" was achieved, the *Volkszeitung-Vorwaerts*-Hillquit crowd had some very tough sledding. Among the prospective joiners in a would-be united "Socialist" party were the Debs and Victor Berger Social Democrats, and both Debs and Berger looked askance at the Eastern contingent of "bourgeois Socialism." Debs charged that the Hillquit crowd was "fairly saturated with the virus of hate and contempt" toward the Midwestern Social Democrats.

"Hundreds of them," said Debs, "members of the anti-De Leon party, and I speak advisedly, still rankle with that feeling which, to even the superficial observer, is but illy concealed." And he added: "It is this sort of training in the school of intolerance, fanaticism and hate which has given the [Hillquit] party a spirit irreconcilably in conflict with that of the Social Democratic [Debs-Berger] party which by its high-minded [!] toleration has appealed so successfully [!] to the American people in behalf of Socialism that its complete supremacy as the Socialist party was only a question of months, while at every step of its progress its [the Social Democratic] members were derided as 'half-baked Socialists' by the very men [Hillquit & Co.] who now, we are assured, insist upon union."

This was Debs's way of saying that Hillquit & Co. were not wanted, that the "high-minded" Social Democrats could get along very well without the "low-minded" Eastern fellows, and it was bitter medicine for the latter to swallow. For Debs here correctly charged Hillquit & Co. with the very vices that they had falsely and slanderously charged against De Leon and the Marxist S.L.P.!

Berger was equally hostile and inhospitable toward the New York lawyer and his friends and dupes. Scathingly Berger fulminated (with particular reference to the *Volkszeitung* outfit):

"In 1889, they [the *Volkszeitung*] had peaceable Germans to fight, who were not prepared for war.[5] But this time they got hold of the wrong fellow. Dan [Daniel De Leon] was prepared, and when the *Volkszeitung's* crowd came to commit 'the revolution' they found a picked lot of Irishmen and Americans to receive them. Dan made short work of the *Volkszeitung-Garde,* and the only fruit of the great revolution for the *Volkszeitung* is the capture of the Labor Lyceum Saloon. Not only this, Daniel De Leon beat them in the courts. He got the Party name and the Party emblem. And what's worse, he also beat them at the following state election: his party [the S.L.P.] receiving about as many votes without the *Volkszeitung's* crowd as with them."

Berger, who was quite as unscrupulous as Hillquit,

---

[5] The reference is to a previous split in the SocialistIC Labor Party, which resulted in the so-called Rochester faction.

but a shrewder politician and given to the use of plain language, assailed the Eastern lawyers, preachers and assorted scribblers unmercifully. Job Harriman (of "De Leon-Harriman Debate" fame) was called a "Tammany politician of the seventeenth degree," James Carey (of Haverhill, Mass., armory appropriation fame) was called a "ward politician," and Morris Hillquit was decorated with the very appropriate label —"a thorough classconscious lawyer of New York"! Lawyers as a class do have their own peculiar kind of "classconsciousness"!

The other side, however, was not found wanting when it came to trading epithets. Max Hayes, a typical craft union defender, to whom De Leon always referred as "Mamie" Hayes, attacked the Social Democratic contingent as "anti-unionists" and spoke of them derogatorily as "intellectuals":

"The anti-unionists [said Hayes] were marshaled by [Victor] Berger, a school teacher and editor; [Seymour] Stedman, a lawyer; McCartney, a preacher; Edwards, another editor; London, still another lawyer; Margaret Haile, a lachrymose woman [!], and one or two others—all so-called academic Socialists, theorists."

Turn about is fair play, so a Berger man, the editor of the *Social Democratic Herald,* pursued this interesting roll call, to wit:

". . . . We might direct attention to the fact that Harriman is a lawyer and ex-preacher; Hillquit is a lawyer; Schlueter, an editor; Feigenbaum, an editor; Morgan, a lawyer; Jonas, an editor; Stone, an editor; Sissman, a lawyer; Benham, an editor; Taft, a lawyer; Lee [Algernon], an editor; and . . . . Max Hayes himself is an editor. . . ."

I think we must all agree that this was indeed a fine roster for prospective or would-be founders of a supposed party of Socialism in the United States! "Out of their own mouths....," etc. These were the noble souls, the high-minded idealists, the self-sacrificing martyrs who were going out to do battle at Armageddon for the Lord! It seems almost as if these gentry were picked on purpose to prove a De Leonist argument, or to point a De Leonist moral! There they were—the pure in spirit, the exalted ones, who were to show how wrong De Leon and the S.L.P. were, who were to demonstrate how Socialism really was to be achieved in America! And there was poor Hillquit—a hardworking lawyer, ready to sacrifice himself on behalf of the source of his wealth—embarked on an unknown sea, his genius unappreciated, his noble motives misjudged by his future comrades and fellow "bourgeois Socialists"! Well might he say, with Cicero: "I know *from* whom I flee without knowing *to* whom I flee."

And so, on July 29, 1901, at Indianapolis, Ind., the bourgeois "Socialist" party was founded, formed out of the most heterogeneous elements, each pulling in a different direction, each with a different notion as to what Socialism was, but each dedicated to himself and his own fortunes—that, at least, was true of the leaders. But they *were* united on one thing—no "De Leonism" for them, which is to say, no Marxism! Each leader, each faction, left that "unity" convention secure in the belief that now at last the stage was set for business — good *"geschaeft-Sozialismus."* And, being agreed that "De Leonism" (Marxism) was anathema, all hoped, or instinctively felt, that never again would they be disturbed by that dread specter! But how wrong they were, as subsequent events fully demonstrated, and as the eventual fate of the bourgeois S.P. sorrowfully brought home to them or their survivors!

9

The S. P.
"Feels Its Oats"

It would seem that even the non-Socialist would have concluded that out of this amorphous mass, or, at any rate, heterogeneous aggregation, nothing but confusion and chaos could ensue.

To the observing Marxist it was certainly patent that, however this new party might fare initially, however successful (in a purely quantitative sense) it might become and remain for a longer or shorter period, it was foredoomed to failure so far as "capturing" the workers for Socialism was concerned. As De Leon put it: "The S.P.'s. . . . downfall is inevitable."

Having put itself athwart the path of revolutionary Socialism to begin with, the S.P. was bound ever to remain an obstacle to the growth of the genuine Socialist movement in America; bound to serve capitalist interests whether it willed it or no; bound to become a thing of ill fame and reproach with all honest, decent men. Conceived in corruption; born in hatred, malice and petty envy; and reared in an atmosphere polluted with the fumes arising from its ill-smelling deals with capitalist interests and capitalist politicians, and from the putrid, fast decomposing body of craft unionism, topped by the stench of its own inner corruption—with all this, what possible prospect could there be in store for this hybrid monstrosity other than decline and fall and eventual extinction?

However, at the outset everything seemed rosy, and "bourgeois Socialist" reform hopes soared. But, as the Old World saying has it, "How long, alas, was Adam in Paradise?" Within a few years the forces of disintegration had already begun their work—heterogeneity asserted its law, the elements that in logic *could* not mix *would* not do so, and these discordant factions were soon tearing each other to pieces and their party asunder. For, inasmuch as the bourgeois S. P. was based on a false principle and on a fraudulent premise, it could neither serve its avowed Socialist purpose, nor discharge fully or satisfactorily its assigned, or intended, mission as a buffer party of capitalism. For to do the latter it would have to maintain its *appearance* as a party of Socialism without the danger of its really becoming one. And since this party revealed itself more and more as a fraud and an object of derision, it was no longer useful — or became less and less so—to capitalist interests. Its law of existence being quantity and material success, pure and simple, reverses that, in a soundly based and logically poised Socialist organization, would have meant merely temporary setbacks became in its case crushing defeats, and marked the beginning of the end. It could not have been otherwise. Attempting to be all things to all men, it was soon reduced to the status of being nothing to anybody.

To such an extent did the S.P. finally degrade itself that in 1932 the "Socialist" party granted a charter in Cook County to a group of Catholics! The point is not that Catholics were admitted to a supposed party of Socialism, but that they were admitted as a group, *as a Catholic branch!* And with the official blessing of the hierarchy! The story is told in an article published in the Milwaukee *Leader* (Berger's paper), in the issue of March 25, 1932. Here it is:

"Party Charter Is Granted to Catholic Group
(Special to the *Leader*)

"Chicago—The Socialist party of Cook County, Illinois, recently granted a branch charter to a group of Catholic Socialists who had applied to the national Socialist party headquarters here for recognition, Clarence O. Senior, national secretary of the Socialist party, disclosed today.

"This is the first Catholic branch to be recognized by the Socialists which is also sanctioned by church officials.

"The recent encyclical of the Pope against Socialism referred to European Socialists only, it was stated by church officials who granted church members the permission to join the Socialist party.

"Many members of the American Catholic clergy have been active in the promotion of progressive thought for several past years."

To such depths of infamy had the bourgeois S.P. sunk that by admitting this Catholic branch, the Berger-Hillquit-Thomas politicians gave tacit approval to the Pope's medieval condemnation of European Socialists! And let it be noted that Norman Thomas was then one of the leading S.P. politicians, being the party's presidential candidate that year!

The "bourgeois Socialist" campaign of 1900 was a confusing one, yet withal revealing as a foreshadowing of what was to follow. A "joint" ticket was nominated, headed by Eugene V. Debs (of the "Social Democrats") as candidate for President and Job Harriman (of the Hillquit-*Volkszeitung* element) as candidate for Vice President. Thus, while within their own circles they fought like hungry dogs, calling each other all sorts of names, outwardly they presented a "united front"—ostensibly against capitalism, but in reality against Marxism and De Leonism. In view of the claims made by these reformers of capitalism, the vote polled by them was insignificant, only somewhat over 96,000. It was a sore disappointment to the hopefuls who had dreamed of votes for the S. P. mounting up to six figures!

A later "Socialist" party writer optimistically wrote of the Indianapolis "unity" convention that "it was made up almost entirely of young men, full of life and vigor, rich with promise, and determined to set America on fire." In view of the fact that the new party was completely dominated by the GERMAN *Volkszeitung* and the JEWISH *Forward* crowds of the East, and by the element clustering around the GERMAN-born Berger in the Midwest (with Debs playing practically no policy-making role), this statement was, to say the least, a slight exaggeration! And as for setting America on fire, the vigor with which the discordant elements within the party threw "cold water" on each other's proposals made setting anything on fire a hopeless undertaking.

At the early stage the chief bones of contention in the S.P. were reform measures ("immediate demands"), the farmer question and the trade union question. Writing in *International Socialist Review* (at that time a mildly unorthodox S.P. monthly) as early as November, 1902, Debs commented:

"There seems to be considerable misapprehension, especially among Socialists, in regard to the trade union movement of the Western states, whose delegates, recently assembled in National Convention,....pledged the support of their organization to the international Socialist movement. This radical departure from *the effete and reactionary non-political policy of the American Federation of Labor,* so long and so earnestly striven for by the Western leaders, *and so entirely compatible with the Socialist conception of classconscious and progressive trade unionism,* should have been met with the prompt and hearty approbation of every unionist *and every Socialist in the land.* That such was not the case, the lukewarm comment and the half-approving, half-condemning tone of the Socialist party press...bear convincing testimony..." (Our italics.)

Poor, naive Debs! Could he really have believed that the pro-capitalist union defenders who had fled from the "De Leonist tyranny" on this question would now submit to a "Debs tyranny" on the identical question? With the delicious odor of the A. F. of L. fleshpots in their nostrils, the Hillquit-Berger-*Volkszeitung-Forward* element would naturally answer Debs, as in effect they did, with a thunderous NO!

Similarly with the question of "immediate demands." At this early stage a number of those who had fought De Leon most bitterly made a great show of opposing reform measures. After all, a decent interval had to pass before they could abandon the pretenses for their revolt against "De Leonism." Others were not under the same compulsion. Thus Seymour

Stedman, a lawyer and a Debs man, wrote in the *International Socialist Review,* July, 1902:

"To say that we must oppose these reform demands until the Socialist party has complete control of the city, state and nation [!] is to become impractical, and leave no program for a possible elected candidate, and the conceit of it will breed sterility, and make De Leon the true Messiah."

Banquo's ghost would not down! "De Leonism" haunted them in their waking and sleeping hours. It became a guide (in reverse) for all their future action. Is De Leon in favor of a certain thing? Down with it! Does De Leon oppose this or that? We're for it! Well could De Leon say, as he did say, "Impossible for a movement to succeed that is based on the hatred for one man."

10

The S. P. "Revolutionists" and the I. W. W.

A few years later (April, 1905) the editor of the *International Socialist Review,* A. M. Simons, wrote: "For some time there have been two extreme camps within the Socialist party. . . . the so-called Opportunists and [the] Impossibilists." The "Impossibilists," according to "bourgeois Socialism," are identifiable as those who (consciously or unconsciously) are "addicted" to "De Leonism." The S.P. editor charged that De Leon was casting "his eyes toward the Socialist party for which he had hitherto had nothing but foul abuse and falsification." ("Abuse" and "falsification" were the gentleman's semantics for "truth" and "logic.") And he added that "rumors came from all over the country that certain groups of 'impossibilists' within the Socialist party were considering affiliation with the S.L.P."

This was written on the eve of the launching of the original I.W.W. And with the appearance of that organization real trouble started in the bourgeois "Socialist" party. It is noteworthy that most of the signers of the call for the Chicago convention were members or sympathizers of the S.P., and they included such S.P. diehards and De Leon-haters as A. M. Simons, Ernest Untermann and others, besides Eugene V. Debs, "Mother" Jones and William D. Haywood.

The only S.L.P. member who signed the call was

Frank Bohn (De Leon was, of course, ignored), who served as National Secretary of the Socialist Labor Party for a short while, deserting it in 1907. He joined the S.P. immediately thereafter, and was welcomed with open arms. His "credentials"? The usual ones: De Leon was a pope, a tyrant, etc., etc.!

It was not long before Bohn found himself with the so-called "left wing" of the S.P. (the "Impossibilists"), which centered around Charles H. Kerr's monthly magazine, the *International Socialist Review*. There was, in fact, no sharp cleavage in the S.P., for the *International Socialist Review* group included such "bourgeois Socialist" wheelhorses as A. M. Simons (one of the editors), Max ("Mamie") Hayes, the lawyer Boudin (who used to write long and tedious theses on "Marxian economics," etc.), Ernest Untermann, Carl D. Thompson ("municipal Socialism" expert), and others. And later we find in that group William D. Haywood, Frank Bohn, William E. Bohn, Debs, and many others.

With the formation of the I.W.W. this magazine became openly critical of the "pure and simple" politicians (Hillquit, Berger, Spargo, *et al.*), and equally vociferous in its acclaim of "industrial unionism." However, whenever they would become too annoying in their criticism, and when it might appear as if they were ready to accept the whole body of S.L.P. teachings, the party's machine politicians, "right" or "left," would raise the specter of "De Leonism," and the name "De Leon" would resound through the whispering galleries of the party, and that would usually have a restraining or "sobering" effect on the recalcitrant elements.

Among the S.P. "intelligentsia" it was considered fatal to be discovered to be (or accused of being) in the least degree tainted with De Leonism. As we know, the name of Trotsky is anathema in Stalinist circles today, and for a Stalinist to be called a Trotskyist is to be libeled in the highest degree and to become a fit subject for liquidation. But even more frightful, and utterly ruinous to a promising career, was it for a member of the S.P. "intelligentsia" ("right" or "left") to be called a "De Leonist." Hence, despite the repeated obituaries pronounced over the S.L.P. and De Leon, both "sparked" practically all the important councils and deliberations of the S.P. Never were there livelier ghosts!

While, then, this so-called left-wing element in the S.P. acclaimed the I.W.W., they did so at first with somewhat muted strings, and generally great efforts were put forth to demonstrate that there was nothing incompatible, on the one hand, in upholding the I.W. W., with its explicit condemnation of the A. F. of L., and, on the other hand, in supporting the S.P. with its "bourgeois Socialist" program and its endorsement and support of the A. F. of L. and kindred unions. Right along the bourgeois "Socialist" party had declared a "neutrality" attitude toward the union question. It is well known that all who in a great contest declare themselves neutral are, in fact, on the side of the enemy. And so it was with the S.P. officialdom on the craft union question. Their would-be pro-Socialism, issuing from one side of the mouth, would be "neutralized" by the pro-capitalist union apologies issuing from the other side. As for their general attitude toward the I.W.W., they would at most (with Alexander Pope),

"Damn with faint praise, assent with civil leer,
And, without sneering, teach the rest to sneer."

A. M. Simons, writing in the *International Socialist Review,* August, 1905, posed the question this way:

"There has been much discussion about what attitude the Socialist party should take toward this new
organization [I.W.W.]. *I cannot see that it is called
upon to act officially in any manner whatever."*

Bear in mind that Simons was one of the founders
of the I.W.W.—one of the signers of the "call"—and
then reflect on his plea for the ostrich act, which in
fact was nothing but a plea for "neutrality"! And this
within a month of the founding of the I.W.W.!

11

Wobbly Anarchism Welcomed by the S. P.

On the whole, however, the official attitude was one of open hostility toward the I.W.W. so long as that organization adhered to the Marxist, that is, the De Leonist position. If anything good might be said about the new revolutionary union, it was played down in the S.P. press. But no opportunity was lost to play up mistakes, and the S.P. papers were for the greater part filled with lies, half-truths and sneers about the I.W.W., always with some reference to the evil one himself, Daniel De Leon! Max Hayes and A. M. Simons (two of the most inveterate De Leon revilers) outdid each other in pouring vitriolic slander on De Leon's head. Max Hayes, writing in the *International Socialist Review*, September, 1905, furnished this choice example of the slander indulged in by the envenomed De Leon-haters:

"From a fourth direction [wrote Hayes] we are forced to meet the hostility of those [De Leonists] who have fed upon their hatred for individuals and organizations to such an extent that they have become unbalanced and run amuck and would now down everybody but those who follow them [!]. I refer to that peculiar band of fanatics that have become generally known as deleonites [sic]. . . . . Captained by a crafty conspirator—who has been a howling failure in the

Single Tax movement, the old K. of L., in the so-called Socialist Trade and Labor Alliance, and who has all but ruined the old Socialist Labor Party of membership and vote polled—this scattered band of disruptionists take peculiar delight in denouncing and vilifying the 'pure and simple Socialists' above all others...

"They have obstinately and blindly butted their heads against a stone wall so persistently that they were practically out of existence, when suddenly the Chicago conference is held and they succeed in engrafting themselves upon the new *Industrial Workers of the World,* and now they are actually making the claim that their methods have been endorsed and with their accustomed brazenness are asserting their right to lead the whole show.

"Back about ten years ago, when Prof. De Leon launched his freak Socialist Trade and Labor Alliance, the edict soon went forth that every Socialist in a trade union who refused to fall upon his knees and worship the new calf [!] was a traitor, a faker, and should be 'kicked out.'

"Now the fellow [De Leon] has the impudence to renew his ridiculous and bombastic command, and whosoever refuses to withdraw from the trade unions and join the 'Industrialists' becomes an object of suspicion . . . . Talk about intrigue and double-dealing to sow the seeds of dissension! The adventurous professor [De Leon] is a past master at the game, and it seems that a great many thoughtless and unsophisticated union men and Socialists are mere putty in his grasp.

"The day that De Leon has long prayed for has come at last. The Socialist party can be split! . . . . I repeat that the day that this cold-blooded schemer has longed for has arrived. *Already in a score of places dissension has developed in the Socialist party, and we find our own members parroting the phrases coined by De Leon a dozen years ago, writing articles for his disreputable organ, and attempting to revive his malevolent and repudiated policies."* (Italics ours.)

And A. M. Simons, then editor of the *International Socialist Review,* unburdened himself of these libels and vilifications in the July, 1907, issue of the S. P. monthly. Under the title, "The Work If Not the Pay of a Spy," the wretch wrote in part:

"Taking all these things [De Leon's exposures of labor faker corruption, and his fight against the bourgeois S.P. politicians] into consideration, the conclusion seems almost [!] inevitable that De Leon is playing the part of a capitalist spy in the Socialist ranks." And the scoundrel proceeded: "There is another feature that leads to the conclusion that he is not doing this unrewarded. He has been running a daily paper in New York for seven years. Although it is little more than a handbill [!], yet with the limited (!) circulation which he has it must have a considerable deficit."

Rising to a Wagnerian crescendo, the slanderer howled: "WHO PAYS THAT DEFICIT? In all these seven years he never made a financial report. It would at least be interesting to see such a report. It might show that he was getting the money as well as doing the work of capitalism."

Except to say that it was not De Leon's function to issue financial reports (they were prepared and furnished to the membership by the business manager, as the lying rascal Simons well knew)—except for that, no further comments are required on this villainous

71

piece of libelous mendacity. And this from the creature who later sold out to capitalist interests!

These self-revealing lampoons by two of the most unprincipled of the "socialistic" craft union apologists are more than "documents in madness." They are howls of anguish, of frustration, of savage-childish acknowledgment of defeat. Their recognition of De Leon's intellectual power and potency is far more significant than the billingsgate and venom with which they overflow. They are not so much a call for action by the embattled S.P. lawyers, parsons and craft union pensioners as they are cries of fear and despair.

Meanwhile the assaults against the Industrial Workers of the World continued, both from within and from without. The anarcho-syndicalist element in the I.W.W. grew bolder, their attacks on De Leon increased in virulence, and in these they were aided by the S.P. politicians who hoped that this would be the end of De Leon as well as of the I.W.W. In justice to Debs it must be said that he had no part in these doings. Debs had been opposed to the physical force elements, although he failed to take an active part in the fight to preserve the Socialist character of the organization, and in effect gave moral support to its enemies.

Finally in 1908 the anarchists and the anarcho-syndicalists succeeded in capturing the I.W.W. Emasculating the once promising revolutionary Socialist union by striking from the preamble the political clause, and fastening the black flag of anarchism to their masthead, they sallied forth to the tunes of "Strike at the ballot box with an ax," and "Halleluja, I'm a bum!" preaching sabotage, "private expropriation" (petty theft), and chanting in chorus: "Down with politics! Down with De Leon!" They practiced what they preached, and made the once honored name of the I.W.W. a designation and symbol of infamy to all decent workers. But, and this is the point, a shout of jubilation went up from the S.P. camp when the I.W.W. was wrecked as a Socialist union. To the "bourgeois Socialists" only one thing was important: "De Leon has been licked"—or so they fondly imagined!

In their exuberance they now (for a while at least) took the wrecked I.W.W. to their bosom. Now their papers were filled with reports of the activities of the anarchist "I.W.W.," and the doings of the murderers of Socialist Industrial Unionism. Men like Haywood, the Bohns, Vincent St. John, and many others, came into national party prominence. "Big Bill" Haywood (who later played an important part in the anarcho-syndicalist I.W.W.) was at this time still in an Idaho prison, and apparently kept aloof from the struggle. The Haywood spirit, however, guided those who finally succeeded in emasculating the I.W.W. preamble. For a while after his release from jail Haywood's primary interest seemed to be to ingratiate himself with the S.P. membership, and he succeeded to the extent of getting himself elected a member of the National Executive Committee of the party. But before very long he revealed himself in his true colors. In 1910, though still calling himself a "Socialist," he declared that "striking out the political clause from the [I.W. W.] preamble was (perhaps) the best that could have been done under the conditions." This mealy-mouthed statement reflected his desire to reconcile his Socialist pretensions with his real sentiments and convictions, which in reality were anarcho-syndicalist, as events soon proved. By 1912 he had sunk so low that he lent his efforts to the breaking of the Paterson strike, until then conducted successfully by the De Leonist ("Detroit") I.W.W.. The injection of Haywood and his "Bummery" I.W.W. into the Paterson-Passaic strike caused confusion and dismay among the strikers, resulting in their eventual defeat.

Prior to the disruption of the Socialist I.W.W. De Leon had looked upon Haywood hopefully as one who might save the organization from destruction. In a letter written to him in 1907, De Leon said:

"We are again in the days when the Republican party was organized out of warring free-soil and abolitionist, and of up to then wavering elements. Thanks to your own antecedents, your celebrated case, the unanimity of the working class in your behalf, and your triumphant vindication, the capitalist class has itself hatched out the needed leader. The capitalist class has thrown the ball into your hands. You can kick it over the goal. . . . Upon the wisdom of your acts it now depends whether the ball is to be kicked over the goal within an appreciable time, or not. The S.L.P., of which it has been slanderously said [that it] is run by one man, myself, just because it is a self-directing body, is sane enough to listen with respectful attention (even though it may disagree) to one who has so long filled my post in its ranks. My individual efforts may be relied upon by you, if you desire them, toward the work that circumstances have combined to cut out for you."

But again De Leon was to be bitterly disappointed, as he had been disappointed in men so often before. However, to resume the story after the 1908 debauch of the I.W.W. and the "unholy," though temporary, alliance between the anarcho-syndicalist and the S.P. politicians:

Frank Bohn (ex-S.L.P. national secretary), whose brother, William E. Bohn, had been spitting the reddest of red in the *International Socialist Review,* co-authored with Haywood a pamphlet on "Industrial Socialism," while carrying on valiantly in the cause of anarcho-syndicalism. Before his exit from the S.L.P. Frank Bohn joined in a conspiracy with the Ultramontane-inspired James Connolly to oust De Leon as S.L.P. editor. Connolly may or may not have been a paid tool of the Catholic political machine (as was frequently charged), but if he did his villainous work voluntarily, he fully earned the gratitude of the Ultramontanes, and of the capitalist class generally. He was executed in 1916 for his part in the Easter rebellion in Ireland—the rebellion that eventually resulted in establishing the present Ultramontane-theocratic regime in Ireland (Eire). Frank Bohn (who also nourished editorial ambitions) and Connolly carried on their campaign against De Leon and the Party in characteristic underground fashion, seeking to poison the minds of the S.L.P. membership against De Leon, and with no small measure of success, though short shrift was made of them and their fellow-conspirators after their treason was fully revealed. Frank Bohn's subsequent career was the logical one—from S.L.P. traitor to anarcho-syndicalist to warmonger and super-patriot!

During the first world war "Frankie" Bohn joined the Wilson crusaders in "the war to save democracy for the world." He specialized in long and tedious patriotic essays printed on the editorial page of the New York *Times* and crowned his career by marrying the daughter of a member of the President's cabinet! William E. Bohn (pardon, "Dr." Bohn) is now a pantalooned and slippered old "liberal" who edits the reactionary anti-Socialist sheet, *The New Leader*. He usually drools about his past (with occasional lying and sneering references to De Leon and the S.L.P.)—his respectable past, that is, for never does he give any inkling of having once been a comrade-in-arms of the anarchist Haywood, with whom he declaimed, for example, that "Whenever there is a strike or lockout or the drawing up of an agreement [sic], the real struggle for the revolution is on." ("R-r-r-revolution," that is!!) A reprinting of the articles he wrote in the *International Socialist Review* would now be greatly embarrassing to him. Or would it?[6] After all, these fellows are thick-skinned, and generally solve all embarrassing situations with a sneer at De Leon and a lie about the S.L.P.

However, the "old guard" in the S.P. soon woke

---

[6] The following is a sample of "Dr." William E. Bohn's "r-r-revolutionary" rantings as he expressed them in the "International Socialist Review," September, 1909, in an article entitled "Reformer and Revolutionist":

"In order to convince ourselves that this is at bottom the distinction between our two tendencies ["reform" and "revolution"] we shall merely have to recall a few [bourgeois] Socialist speeches or articles. Is not your reformer always telling us that all we need is a majority of the votes? Does he not calm our minds with the assurance that we can 'get Socialism' little by little; pass now one law, now another, take over first this industry then that under government control? And your revolutionist [**that's me, Bill Bohn!**] —is he not always talking of the class struggle, of strikes and lockouts? Does he not represent the advent of Socialism as the result of a **bitter physical fight,** a fight quite beyond control of the State?" (Bold face mine.) "Dr." Bohn might try that now on his 1950 Liberal party piano!

See "The Renegade's Compulsion," pages 121-156.

up to the fact that they had bedded with a bobcat, or a reasonable facsimile thereof. Within a few years the party of "bourgeois Socialism" was internally rent in twain, though its membership and vote increased steadily, reaching their peak in 1912. During the year 1910 a violent feud raged between the "roughnecks" and the "intelligentsia," though again it must be noted that the cleavage was not sharp. For among the "roughnecks" there were "intellectuals," and the latter had their share of "roughnecks." A typical outburst by a rank-and-file "roughneck" is contained in a letter written by one of them to the *International Socialist Review*. The letter throws light on the practices of the petty bourgeois "Socialists" in the S.P. Here is what it said, in part:

"Fellow industrial proletarians, what shall we do with the 'educated Socialists' and the 'respectable Socialists'? . . . . We must remand them to the rear or repudiate them if we want to establish the Industrial Republic. . . . Behold the Socialist movement in the United States today [1909]! It is really in a deplorable state of confusion. One day the cry is 'Votes for Women,' the next day 'Down with Hinky Dink,' the next, 'Hurrah for 3-cent fares,' 'Down with the Japs,' and the rest of the incessant nonsense that has emanated from our 'leaders.' We do not want benevolent feudalism; we want Socialism."

This, generally, was the cry of the "overall brigade," and it increased steadily in volume. Local Denver, S.P., issued a loud blast, which the editor of the S.P. monthly thought was important enough to publish in full under the heading, "What Is the Matter with the Socialist Party?" It was in the form of a resolution addressed to the membership of the party. It opened with a declaration that "the Socialist party of the United States is not a revolutionary organization of the working class. . . . but is merely a stamping ground for faddists, careerists and notoriety seekers bent upon obtaining pelf and power at the expense of an already overburdened class." It continued:

"Practically all of the official positions in this organization have been usurped by as conscienceless a crew of bourgeois buccaneers as ever practiced piracy on the high seas of Liberty, Equality and Fraternity . . . . This cockroach element, composed of preachers without pulpits, lawyers without clients, doctors without patients, storekeepers without customers, disgruntled political coyotes and other riffraff . . . has relegated the real proletarians to the rear. . . . "

It concluded by denouncing, in De Leonist terms, the "mad scramble for votes" and "such infamies" as "craft unionism," "anti-immigration," "state autonomy" and "a series of ludicrous and illogical 'immediate demands,' " etc., etc.

12

The S. P. Has Become
A "Hissing and a Byword"

In the year 1910 a major explosion took place within the bourgeois "Socialist" party. It was set off by the publication (in the *International Socialist Review,* January, 1910) of a letter written by A. M. Simons to one William English Walling, an author who subsequently joined the S.P., and who later deserted it as a war patriot to join the Wilson crusaders during the first world war. The letter written to Walling (published by Walling without Simons' consent or prior knowledge) had been prompted by what Mr. Simons had recently witnessed and heard while on tour. In his letter Mr. Simons observed that "The most pitiful thing about the situation is the intense hatred against the Socialist party *combined with a perfect willingness to accept the philosophy of Socialism.*"

This observation by one of the most inveterate foes of Marxian-De Leonist Socialism throws a brilliant searchlight on the "bourgeois Socialism" that was the heart of the S.P. For ten years that party had propagated its brand of "Socialism"; it had been widely advertised by the capitalist press during these years, and had received, and accepted, the praise bestowed upon it by capitalist spokesmen who lauded it and its leading lights as "sane," "reasonable" and "practical." And all this in order to catch votes, particularly to get the support of "union labor." Yet, at the end of the decade the party was derided and rejected by the very people who sincerely wanted Socialism, by those who logically should acclaim it, but who had found that they would have to achieve their hearts' desire in spite of the S.P., and by methods diametrically opposed to those of the S.P.

Thus the iron logic of events asserted itself, and De Leonism (Marxism) received its vindication, aided by the stupidity and avariciousness of the vulgar crowd that had usurped the name of Socialism and traded on it for private profit. For with all their supposed cleverness, these exploiters of the labor movement were fundamentally stupid, although through their very stupidity they served the great purpose of demonstrating to the workers that "bourgeois Socialism" (and its corollary, craft unionism) was their greatest enemy and the greatest obstacle to the achievement of working class emancipation. As Marx once wrote in a letter to Engels: "When God wants to do something especially great, says old Carlyle, he always chooses out the stupidest people for it."

The question, however, was: Should the S.P. be "reformed" or should it be merged with a "Labor party"? Mr. Simons continues in his letter to Walling:

"Now we have two alternatives before us. . . . The first of these. . . . is to *so reform the Socialist party that it will fill the function for which it was intended* . . . . Right here we come to the most delicate portion before us. . . .

"THE S.P. HAS BECOME A HISSING AND A BYWORD WITH THE ACTUAL WAGE WORKERS OF AMERICA. It has become the party of the two extremes. *On the one side are a bunch of intellectuals like MYSELF and Spargo and Hunter and Hillquit, on the other is a bunch of 'never-works,' demagogues and would-be intellectuals, a veritable 'lumpenproletariat.' The actual wage workers, the men who are really FIGHTING the class struggle, are outside."* (Emphases mine.)

The startling frankness of Simons is of course explained by the fact that he wrote the letter in confidence, never suspecting that Walling (at that time a non-party member) would violate his confidence. This circumstance renders the confession of Simons all the more important, revealing as nothing else could have done the depth of the corruption in the S.P.

Simons made a number of additional acknowledgments of the bankruptcy of the "bourgeois Socialist" party and revealed his own attitude in definite terms. Bear in mind that he was one of the founders of the original I.W.W. and an ardent De Leon-hater. Of Industrial Unionism he said (five years after the launching of the I.W.W.) that he thought "its most deadly enemy is the man who talks about it as a means of getting the cooperative commonwealth. *We are not organizing unions in the future or in the past but NOW* [!]...." (Emphases mine.)

And he now comes to the crux of the matter:

"Above all else we MUST have the union men [read, "labor fakers"]. No one has denounced the defects of the A. F. of L. more than I, but I am forced to recognize that *it comes much nearer representing the working class than the S.P.,* and unless we are able to so shape our policy and our organization as to meet the

81

demands and incarnate the position of the workers *we will have failed of our mission.*"

The letter took everyone by surprise. And now the fat was in the fire—the battle was on. Among other things a lengthy epistolary debate followed between Hillquit and S.P. millionaire J. G. Phelps Stokes (published in the *International Socialist Review*), in the course of which each challenged the other's motives and intellectual honesty! The complete details of the story would make fascinating reading and would certainly prove highly instructive. But the telling of that story must be reserved for a future occasion. It is enough to repeat that in the struggle the corrupt party of "bourgeois Socialism" was thrown into internal convulsions and became thoroughly disrupted, even though outwardly it maintained the appearance of a "growing" party.

Eventually, the Hillquit-Simons-Spargo crew emerged from the struggle victorious; though, whether they knew it or not, what they had actually achieved was a Pyrrhic victory. Another and really fatal blow was struck at the S.P. ten years later when (after the first world war) the bulk of its membership deserted it to join what eventually became the Communist party of America. This was of the very essence of logic. The training the S.P. members received in their corrupt party preeminently fitted them for the role they were to play in the equally corrupt and jesuitical "Communist" party. Ignorant as they were of Marxism, the opportunism they were taught by the Hillquits, the unscrupulousness they had practiced in the S.P., all combined to make them ideal subjects, pliable puppets, for the unprincipled gang that presently developed into what we now know as Stalinists. Thus Hillquitism prepared the way for American Stalinism, even as the "Social Democracy" of Germany prepared the way for Hitlerism. In the language of Marx, the logic of things will tell!

And in this last struggle the same or similar charges were hurled at the S.P.—that it was a bourgeois outfit, that it was dominated by the "intellectual riffraff," and by the reactionary craft union leaders, "socialistic" and otherwise, etc., etc.

But in this second "partition" of the S.P. many a familiar face was missing. Many of the "intellectuals" had joined the forces of "righteousness" under the leadership of Woodrow Wilson, practically all of them having developed into war patriots and preachers of social patriotism.

13

A Rogues' Gallery

Outstanding among these were John Spargo, who became a respectable Vermont Republican, whooping it up for Hoover; Robert Hunter, who had been regarded as one of the outstanding S.P. "intellectuals," and who terminated his career (and life) writing a book on "the anatomy of revolution," this apparently being designed as a primer for despairing capitalists who worry too much about the security of their power and privileges as exploiters of labor[7]; A. M. Simons, who ended his "Marxist" career as a consultant to a corporation on "labor troubles," writing essays on how to "handle" labor and "union problems"; Robert Rives La Monte, a one-time "intellectual roughneck," who spent his old age as a respectable Connecticut Yankee, preaching bourgeois morality; Charles Edward Russell, prominent New York "intellectual" and former S.P. candidate for Governor in New York State, another converted Wilson war patriot who got so discouraged

---

[7] Writing as if he were not personally involved, Hunter observed in his book ("Revolution, Why, How, When?"—1940): "Like Frankenstein, 'the scientific Socialists' have been destroyed by their own works. Many Socialists have become apostates in the last quarter of a century." In the same passage he refers to "the days when I was seeing much of the Socialists...."—meaning his "bourgeois Socialist" comrades! He was of the very inner circle, though one of the earliest to turn "apostate" during World War I! Yet this man, in the perfervid manner characteristic of the typical bourgeois "socialist," had written thirty years earlier ("International Socialist Review," April 1909): "Socialism after all is only a matter of time and its coming as certain as the coming of the dawn"!!

that he declared he was going to "raise roses in the country"; William English Walling, also a one-time "roughneck intellectual" turned war patriot; Frank and William E. Bohn, who have already been catalogued; William J. Ghent, systematic De Leon-hater, another "intellectual," whose chief claim to fame after he climbed on the Wilson bandwagon was the writing of a book, which—revealingly—he called "The Reds Bring Reaction"; J. G. Phelps Stokes, millionaire "Socialist," who had married a poor East Side girl, and who specialized as a "social uplifter," and who also turned war patriot, divorcing his wife when she became a "Communist"; Walter Lippmann, at one time secretary to S.P. Mayor George Lunn of Schenectady (Lippmann is now serving as chief plutogogic apologist; Lunn, now dead, turned Democratic politician); S.P. Mayor Hoan of Milwaukee, who joined the Democratic party; Andrew Biemiller, also a prominent S.P. office holder in Milwaukee, now Congressman elected on the Democratic party ticket; and a host of others, similarly constituted, who terminated their "bourgeois Socialist" careers in like fashion.

The careers of Hoan and Biemiller are characteristic "case histories" of a much later date, and they illustrate beautifully the corruption and bourgeois nature of the "Socialist party," confirming the contention of Marxian Socialists that this party of "bourgeois Socialism" has served (and, within its present limitations, still serves) as the hatchery for the breeding of lackeys of capitalism. In a full-page article on Bergerism by Walter Wyrick in the Milwaukee *Journal* of May 12, 1940, the following brief sketch of Hoan is given:

"Dan Hoan, fresh from Chicago, in his first campaign speech when he was running for city attorney, delivered a straight Marxian [?] talk.

"After the meeting, [S.P. Mayor] Seidel, who had listened patiently, took Hoan aside.

" 'Say, young fellow,' Seidel exclaimed, 'what's the idea? You're running against a fellow named Kelley. The idea is to start raising hell with Kelley.'

"Hoan took the hint and was elected."

Hoan "took the hint," no doubt about it! He took it so well that later he was elected Mayor of Milwaukee (again and again), and proved a most efficient administrator of capitalist interests. But he continued to be hailed by his fellow reformers in the S.P. as a "good Socialist." Norman Thomas, in *The Call*, April 27, 1940, wrote:

"We Socialists know that not only has he [Hoan] given the best administration in the country, *but that he has kept his Socialist loyalty and his Socialist faith.*"

Shortly thereafter Hoan was repudiated by the county central committee of the S.P., and in 1944 he ran for Governor of Wisconsin on the Democratic ticket. He was, of course, defeated. Oh, yes, he had indeed "kept his [bourgeois] Socialist loyalty and his [bourgeois] Socialist faith"—and with a vengeance! S.P. State Secretary Frank Zeidler (brother of Mayor Carl Zeidler) cheerfully remarked that "Big business finally got Mayor Hoan. . . ." As if "big business" hadn't had him all the time! Speaking of the corrupt political trading between the Wisconsin S.P. politicians and the Progressive party politicians, Norman Thomas (admitting that he had approved of the "deal" in 1935) ruefully observed: "I am sorry it did not work. Riding two horses does not work. So we are back on the Socialist horse." Odd that Mr. Thomas should not have been able to distinguish between a horse and a donkey!

The story of Biemiller's career is similar. He came to public notice in 1932 when he became active in Norman Thomas's campaign for President. Later he went to Milwaukee to serve as "educational director," and subsequently as editor of the now defunct Milwaukee *Leader,* local S.P. newspaper founded by Victor Berger. In 1935 a coalition was formed between the La Follette Progressive party and the "Socialist" party, and when this broke up Biemiller emerged as a "Progressive" leader in the Wisconsin assembly. Together with Hoan and other "bourgeois Socialists" he joined the so-called Farmer Labor Progressive Federation. When ordered by the S.P. to withdraw from the Federation, Hoan, Biemiller and the others ignored the order and were subsequently "read out" of the S.P. The "expulsion" of Biemiller was announced in the following statement by the county central committee of the S.P.:

"At present the status of Andrew Biemiller in the Socialist party is that of an inactive member, since he has not sent in his notice of intention to remain with the Socialist party [!!]. In such a position, he cannot be subject to the discipline of the Socialist party, and the Socialist party does not hold itself responsible for his present activities"!

In 1941 the Roosevelt Administration rewarded Biemiller with an appointment to the Office of Production Management at a salary of $4,600. In logical sequence Biemiller joined the Democratic party, being elected as Democratic Congressman in 1944. Thus again politicians and "intellectuals" of the S.P., with relentless logic, performed in accordance with the law of existence of "bourgeois Socialism," as they and their kindred will continue to do to the final end. Even as this is being written it is announced that Jasper Mc-Levy, S.P. Mayor of Bridgeport, has accepted the endorsement of the ultra-reactionary Vivian Kellems and her so-called Independence party. The witless National Secretary of the S.P. (one Fleischman) tearfully wrote to the New York *Post* (August 23, 1950) that "we [bourgeois] Socialists are extremely unhappy over Bridgeport's Socialist [!] Mayor Jasper McLevy's acceptance of the endorsement of Miss Kellems' Independence party." Norman Thomas was terribly upset and said that "Of course further action must be taken in this situation. . . . This is in violation of the Socialist party's constitution." Tsch! tsch! tsch! "If "further action" (disciplinary) has been taken, Thomas & Co. have managed to keep it a pretty dark secret! A slap on the wrist is indicated, and Mr. Jasper McLevy will pursue the even tenor of his way, faithfully serving capitalist class interests in Bridgeport.

In every important respect they confirmed De Leon's dictum on "intellectuals": "The 'intellectuals' see in Socialism only an opportunity for tilts of wit. They don't take the movement seriously. From that attitude to corruption there is hardly a span." Debs on the one side, and Hillquit on the other, stuck to the S.P., but neither could have had any illusions about the future of their corrupt and bankrupt party.

To return to the 1910 eruption: Debs, in a letter to Walling (published in the *International Socialist Review*, January, 1910), once again had denounced his own party, acknowledging "the tendencies to *reaction*" in the S.P., and crying that "A HALT WILL HAVE TO BE CALLED," concluding: "If the trimmers had their way, we should degenerate into bourgeois reform." As if the S.P. had not already so degenerated, and as if Debs didn't know it!

Hillquit, of course, defended the bourgeois S.P., but conceded that it was in a bad way, and that it probably would have to encourage a "Labor party" on the British model, adding that the S.P. "could not consistently oppose such an organization, but that it would have to support it and cooperate with it." (*International Socialist Review,* January, 1910.)

With nominal victory fully secured, the Hillquit crowd proceeded with a fixed determination to make the S.P. into a 100 per cent respectable "bourgeois Socialist" party. After all, there were the A. F. of L. fleshpots to consider, and Hillquit did want so badly to be elected to Congress. And he loved to prance and posture before international congresses, though there was abundant evidence to show that he and his associates were generally held in contempt by their European confreres. Hillquit made repeated attempts to get elected to the United States Congress, obviously envying the shrewder politician, Victor Berger, because he beat him to it. During one of his campaigns (in 1908) for this office he was opposed by Daniel De Leon in the same congressional district—and De Leon spared no effort to expose the fraudulent claims of the ambitious lawyer. One of Hillquit's stooges wrote De Leon, pleading with him to desist, since De Leon's campaign spoiled Hillquit's chances of getting elected. De Leon answered the fatuous fellow:

"If my candidature prevents Hillquit's election, then it follows that Hillquit's candidature prevents my election."

There was no comeback to that one!

14

The Heyday Of the S. P.

During the four years that followed the 1910 eruptions in the S.P., the party grew rapidly in votes and members, achieving its greatest strength in 1912. In that year the party claimed a membership of 150,000 and it polled a vote little short of 1,000,000. Hillquit, at the 1912 national convention of the party, boastingly asserted: "The Socialist party has grown into a political party of first magnitude"! With his aptitude for showmanship he declaimed: "Whether the Socialist party [vote] will show up a million and a half or two millions strong will be a historical fact which will lay the foundation for a new society, for a new life in this country." Hillquit was not day-dreaming—sensing the approach of the political graveyard, he was whistling to keep up his courage!

According to the report to the 1912 convention, the S.P. had 1,039 elected officials throughout the country, including two state senators, 145 aldermen, 160 councilmen, 59 judicial officials, 155 school officials, three superintendents of the poor, 56 mayors and four dogcatchers. The report further boasted of approximately 325 periodicals, of which 13 were daily papers and nearly 300 were weekly papers. The party was indeed riding high—and fatedly riding for a fall. For, like "the glory that was Greece, and the grandeur that was

Rome," the "glory" and "grandeur" that were the S.P. "bourgeois Socialism" have utterly vanished, leaving scarcely a trace behind; only an evil smell and a bitter taste.

But, for the nonce, the party was really in business —good, profitable business. And in their eagerness to please everybody, or at least to offend none, the leading politicians went all out in their reform demands, and trimmed their policies as never before, to please the reactionary craft union leaders, and to get elected to political office. On the question of immigration, Hillquit & Co. adopted a completely reactionary stand, both at home and abroad. At the 1910 congress of the Socialist party two reports were submitted, both urging, or ultimately accepting, exclusion of so-called backward races. The majority report (submitted by Victor Berger, Ernest Untermann and Joshua Wanhope) recommended "the unconditional exclusion of these races," the "races" thereupon being identified as "Chinese, Japanese, Koreans and Hindus." The minority report (submitted by John Spargo) tried to straddle the issue, protesting the exclusion of "Orientals," etc., but agreeing in principle with the majority, arguing that if such immigration (of "backward" races) became a menace, then, said Spargo, "the Socialist party would be compelled, however regretfully, to stand for that measure"—that is, for "total exclusion" of alleged backward races!

Hillquit, as usual, tried to steer a middle course. As the S.P. writer, N. Fine, later wrote: "As usual he perceived the significant tendencies of the two sides, and took a centrist position." His compromise motion in fact agreed with the reactionary position of the majority report, but it was presented in typical shyster lawyer fashion to make it appear otherwise. He "denounced" restrictions on immigration, and then endorsed them by saying that he favored congressional legislation "to prevent. . . .mass importation of workers from foreign countries. . . ." The trick worked: his compromise was adopted, but only by a narrow margin. No one could take offense at his proposal, except, of course, the Marxian "Impossibilists." It suited the reactionary craft union leaders, and that was the important consideration. Debs denounced the majority report as "utterly unsocialistic, reactionary, and in truth outrageous." His old pal, Victor Berger (co-author of the majority report), didn't like that at all! [8]

---

[8] By this time Debs and Berger had apparently parted ways, though outwardly they presented themselves as loving comrades! Already at the 1908 S.P. convention Berger had bestowed upon Debs the "kiss of death," when presidential nominations were the order of business. Debs's name had been placed in nomination by an obscure delegate from Missouri, who in his peroration offered "the name of one who is known to us all, our loved and loving comrade, tried and true—Eugene V. Debs, of Indiana."

Berger arose. He was not to be outdone in the "loved and loving" Debs business, even though he was about to knife his former close pal. Said Berger:

"Comrades, I love Eugene V. Debs probably as much as any man or woman here. I have slept with him in the same bed [!] I have eaten with him at the same table. We have drank [sic] from the same glass [!] We have worked faithfully together for the same movement for many years. Our names were coupled together for many years. . . .Until about three years ago [1905—founding of the I.W.W.!] there were not. . . . any two men who were closer friends and comrades than Eugene V. Debs and Victor Berger."

But—

"I name the Honorable Carl D. Thompson"!

Thompson was a Wisconsin politician, supposed "municipal government expert" and an ex-preacher.

Debs received the convention nomination!

Another bone of contention among the "bourgeois Socialists" was the question of "confiscation" or "compensation." The dominant element wanted to buy out the capitalist class, and on this point, as on almost every reactionary measure, they followed the lead of the European Social Democrats, and in particular that of Karl Kautsky. Kautsky was the idol of, and served as the model for, Hillquit, who aped this German Social Democrat in everything. Kautsky, a much overrated personality, had written extensively on Marxism, and had succeeded in turning out a few readable and fairly worthwhile popular works on Marxism. He was, however, like his American disciple, an incorrigible compromiser and trimmer. The net result of his life's work has been to corrupt the movements in many European countries, and, of course, to lend seeming sanction and authority to the corrupt anti-Socialist acts of the American S.P.

When a very young man (in his mid-twenties) Kautsky met Karl Marx in London. The thumbnail sketch Marx drew of him is precious. Marx, with his penchant for giving nicknames to friends and foes, called him "Kauz," which I understand means "queer fellow"! In a letter to his eldest daughter in 1881 (referring to a certain "gossipmonger, Hirsch"), Marx commented: "He [Hirsch] has found a companion in Kautsky—at whom he scowled so darkly; Engels too has taken a much milder view of this Kauz [Kautsky] since he has proved himself a very talented drinker. When this charmer first appeared at my place—I mean little Kauz—the first question which escaped me was: Are you like your mother? Not in the very least, he assured me, and I silently congratulated his mother. He [continued Marx] is a mediocrity with a small-minded outlook, superwise (only 26), very conceited, industrious in a certain sort of way, he busies himself a lot with statistics, but does not read anything very clever out of them, belongs by nature to the tribe of the philistines but is otherwise a decent fellow in his own way [!]. I turn him over to friend Engels as much as possible."

This delightful sketch does full justice to Kautsky as he came to be known later. He possessed all the attributes that would appeal to a vain, shallow, stage-strutting Hillquit.

Writing in the British Independent Labor party quarterly magazine, *The Socialist Review* (April-June 1919), in an article entitled "Expropriation and Confiscation," Kautsky delivered himself of the following:

"For economic reasons, in the interest of the undisturbed continuance of production, it is urgently desirable that the principle should be established of compensation for all those industrial establishments, the owners of which have not made themselves liable to any penalties [!]. We must draw upon the moneybags of the capitalist in order to defray the costs of compensation"—to the capitalists!

Many years earlier (in 1902) Kautsky had already declared: "There are....a number of reasons which indicate that a proletarian regime will seek the road of compensation, and payment of the capitalists and landowners." (Kautsky: "The Social Revolution.")

The fatuousness of the man is almost unbelievable. As if the plutocracy would allow themselves to be fooled by accepting worthless pieces of paper for their property—worthless, that is, if the "Socialists" meant business, *Socialist* business. If they did not, then obviously nothing would have been changed by "buying out" the capitalists, since they would continue to receive their profit, though in a somewhat changed form. And in that case the workers would have been swindled and betrayed, since they would continue to sweat in order to support an idle and useless class—the class from whom they would have "bought" the wealth they (the workers) had themselves produced in the first place!

15

Reactionary Utopians

These and similar reactionary proposals proved beyond question the "bourgeois Socialist" character of the Kautskys and Hillquits and of the so-called Social Democratic parties that they dominated. They fully answered to the description of "bourgeois Socialism" given in the "Communist Manifesto," though they were far less effective in their destructive analyses of capitalism than their ideological ancestors.

"This school of Socialism," Marx and Engels wrote in the "Communist Manifesto," "dissected with great astuteness the contradictions in the conditions of modern production. It . . . . proved incontrovertibly the disastrous effects of machinery and division of labor; the concentration of capital and land in a few hands; overproduction and crises; . . . . the inevitable ruin of the petty bourgeois and peasant, the misery of the proletariat, the anarchy in production, the crying inequalities in the distribution of wealth, the industrial war of extermination between nations . . . .," etc., etc.

"In its positive aims, however, this form of Socialism aspires either to restoring the old means of production and of exchange, and with them the old property relations and the old society, *or to cramping the modern means of production and of exchange within the framework of the old property relations that have been and were bound to be exploded by those means. IN*

EITHER CASE, IT IS BOTH REACTIONARY AND UTOPIAN." (Our italics and capitals.)

"Reactionary" and "utopian" are precisely the terms that fitted the S.P., despite all the protesting Debses (who cheerfully collaborated in maintaining the fraud), and despite the incidental "revolutionary" window trimming with which the "bourgeois Socialist" politicians used to decorate their front in order to soothe the suspicious and cheer the unwary. And all for the purpose of hanging on to the A. F. of L. flesh-pots, and to roll up a large vote.

Incessantly they kept up the cry for votes. "Vote for our candidates, elect us to office, and lo! we will deliver Socialism to you on a silver platter—or maybe even on a golden one!" Persistently they ignored—as in the nature of things they had to ignore—De Leon's warning that the day of political victory of a party of Socialism without the economic (industrial) organization to enforce that victory would be the day of its defeat. Their concept of Socialism was national ownership, state ownership, municipal ownership, mixed with private ownership of small businesses and farms. The latter was designed to attract the petty capitalists, the corner grocers, and similar small-fry exploiters and nondescript bourgeois elements. Hillquit, testifying before the Commission on Industrial Relations in 1914, expounded before this federal committee his notions of Socialism, what it was, and how to get it. Said he:

"The Socialists do not contemplate a complete change of the system in one day.... for that reason, the Socialists work toward the gradual introduction of the Socialist system....

"For instance, we advocate the *national* ownership

of, say, interstate railroads, telephones, telegraph and other means of interstate communication and transportation. We may also conceive the propriety [!] of *national* ownership of mines, or of such industries as are already organized on a national scale....We may, on the other hand, conceive of certain industries wholly located within one state and best managed *by the state government.*

"Then there is the large area of municipal industries....which should be operated, and could be operated most economically [!], and to the best advantage, by the *city....*

"The system of Socialism, *as we understand it* [sic!], does not necessarily exclude the private ownership and management of purely individual industries ....not based on the exploitation of labor...."

This, as we note, is the kind of system known as State capitalism, and the present living example of it is found in Great Britain today, and (with a certain modification) in Stalinist Russia as well. It is hardly necessary here to expose the fraudulent character of this form of "Socialism." It is, however, essentially the classical "bourgeois Socialism" so well analyzed by Marx and Engels, with minor changes in the *form,* but no change whatever in the *essence* of the capitalist or State relationship to the exploited workers. The State and the bureaucracy take the place of the corporate or single capitalist exploiter.

Before the same committee **Mr.** Hillquit affirmed his belief in the Kautskian theory of buying from the robber class the wealth it robbed from the workers. He said: "At present we are in the market for buying out the capitalist." And when Mr. Gompers (who was a member of the committee) asked him how he expected to finance "such a proposition," Mr. Hillquit answered:

"I suppose that, if paid, it will be paid in some government securities"!!

"IF paid," said he—indicating clearly that there would be *no* payment. Thus spoke the double-dealing swindler—or perhaps one should charitably say: Thus spoke the fool in his folly.

However, generally the "bourgeois Socialists" would limit themselves to pure and simple ballot methods—get elected and take over. How? And what would the capitalist owners do in the meantime? Wilhelm Liebknecht (the elder Liebknecht) graphically and mockingly outlined the procedure and its results in a speech he delivered in the German *Reichstag,* which was later released under the title, "As to the political posture of the Social Democracy, especially with regard to the *Reichstag."* Said Liebknecht:

"But let us suppose that the government, either out of conscious strength or calculation, makes no use of its powers, and that, agreeable to the daydream of some Socialist fantastic politicians, the effort of a Social Democratic majority in the *Reichstag* were successful—what is the majority to do? . . . .

"The moment has arrived to remodel the society and the State. The majority adopts a world historic resolution; the New Era is born?—not at all! A company of soldiers chases the Social Democratic majority out of the temple; and, should the gentlemen fail to submit quietly, then a couple of policemen will conduct them to the lockup, where they will have leisure to meditate upon their Quixotism."

That, certainly, is the least that would happen. But

it is far more likely that the criminal folly of the "bourgeois Socialist" politicians would lead to the appearance of the "man on horseback" and a massacre of the working class that had allowed itself to be deluded by the fatuous or crooked politicians.

16

"Bourgeois Socialism" Reaches Its "Peak" In Norman Thomas

The first world war shattered all these illusions for millions of workers the world over. And it shattered the bourgeois S.P. structure, which came crashing down on the heads of the politicians. But not *their* illusions —if that's what they were. At least the Hillquit-Berger-Debs combine professed to be unshaken in their belief in "Socialism"—*their* idea of Socialism.

But the war and its aftermath caused the further disintegration of the party that had boasted of votes, followers, circulation of papers, etc., in terms of millions. As we have seen, most of the "intellectuals" gave up all Socialist pretensions, joined one or the other of the old parties, and supported the war effort, selling war bonds among other things in collaboration with the unsavory W. Z. Foster, the literary buffoon Max Eastman, and their ilk. Thousands of the "horny-handed sons of toil" (mostly from the foreign language federations) joined the anarcho-Communist group then aborning. These so-called "left-wingers" in the S.P. were then captained by a sinister young character named Louis C. Fraina—originally Jesuit-trained, subsequently a member of the S.P., then for a few years a member of the S.L.P., and back again into the S.P. whence, as said, he graduated to "leadership" of the American "Bolsheviki," only to betray and desert these, and to wind up as a respectable "professor" (under an innocuous-sounding alias, "Lewis Corey") at an Ohio college where presently he dispenses capitalist political economy for pay, and (on the side) bourgeois "Socialist" wisdom—for fun? One wonders.

This, then, was the fruit of the treason committed against Marxian Socialism twenty to thirty years earlier by American "bourgeois Socialism." This was the result of the S.P.ers' conspiracies, double-dealing, trickery and betrayal of honest, though deluded, workers. The party, which already in 1910 was derided as a "hissing and a byword with the actual wage workers of America," had by 1920 descended to an even lower level as far as the working class was concerned. It was held in the deepest contempt by "right," "left" and "center," and only a handful remained to shed tears over the bankrupt concern, with a few die-hard politicians scheming to use the discredited thing by fastening it to some avowed bourgeois reform party or other.

Then came 1924, when the straggling survivors of the party attempted to climb on the elder La Follette's bandwagon. La Follette tolerated them, but treated them with contempt. W. Z. Foster and his anarcho-Communist outfit also sought to climb aboard the La Follette vehicle, but that astute politician was no Henry Wallace. He kicked them all over the place, leaving Foster & Co. in no doubt that this was not a case of dissembling his love!

With the fortunes of the S.P. sunk to their lowest level, with all the political jobs gone (including, presumably, those of the four dogcatchers!), with the disappearance of one paper after the other (the New

York *Daily Call* being among the casualties), it would seem that the next thing in order was a decent burial. But just about this time another evangelical hero made his entrance on the stage. It was none other than Norman Thomas, ex-preacher and bourgeois social uplifter. After the demise of the New York *Daily Call,* he and a group around him started the daily *New Leader.* It was a queer and a sorry thing to look at, and did not last long. When Thomas gave up, the paper was turned into a weekly and, as we have already noted, survives today as an undisguised bourgeois liberal "journal of opinion" under the editorship of the erstwhile blood-and-thunder "industrial Socialist," "Dr." William E. Bohn.

After the *New Leader* fiasco Norman Thomas tried his hand at active politics in what remained of the S.P. It seemed to work—and he liked it! He was nominated for the Presidency on the S.P. ticket in 1928 and was regularly renominated every four years, including 1948. Hillquit, who was ailing, and who wielded less and less influence, apparently did not like the "upstart." However, after the deaths of Debs and Hillquit, there was none to dispute the tawdry S.P. crown with Thomas, and he has worn it ever since.

In the mid-thirties it appeared as if Mr. Thomas were prepared to go over to the Stalinist camp. The Stalinists, sensing an opportunity, manifested a "friendly interest," and Mr. Thomas began to denounce reforms—while continuing to preach and practice reformism! Soon the decrepit and decayed S.P. again had a "left wing" and a "right wing"—Mr. Thomas playing the part of "left-wing" leader and Algernon Lee, the *New Leader*-Rand School crowd and allies performing as "right-wingers." Finally the "split" came. Mr. Thomas continued as the *fuehrer* of the moribund S.P. machine, retaining the name "Socialist party," while the "right-wingers" constituted themselves into something they called the "Social Democratic Federation," retaining control of the *New Leader* and the brain-gouging institution, "The Rand School." The "right-wingers" subsequently joined forces openly with the Roosevelt-Farley machine in New York. The "left" and "right" wings (as we shall note presently) are now about to resume political housekeeping together!

The period since the "split," and what has happened in, and to, the S.P., may perhaps be best described as a prolonged wake over the putrid body of the bourgeois "Socialist" party, with Parson Thomas in constant attendance.

The "party" suffered its minor ups and downs during this period, but its vote steadily dwindled until it has now practically reached zero. During the years Thomas has performed in keeping with the principles and policies of "bourgeois Socialism," adding a few novelties of his own now and then. As with his predecessors in the "party," he has been widely advertised by the capitalist press and praised highly by outstanding capitalist spokesmen. And like his predecessors he has complained that the old parties have stolen his platform planks—blissfully oblivious of the fact that by so complaining (and with cause) he acknowledges that his party is, in truth and fact, a bourgeois reform party—a true party of "bourgeois Socialism."[9]

---

[9] In the New York "Times," of June 7, 1936, Mr. Thomas was interviewed by Mr. S. J. Woolf, the artist-journalist. In

This conclusion means that the S.P. is no more a party of Socialism—and never has been—than a mule is a horse! How could it be? As long ago as 1910, Emil Seidel of Milwaukee, the first S.P. man to be elected to the office of mayor in the United States, stated:

"It isn't essential that the workers be instructed in Socialism. It doesn't make any difference whether the workers understand Socialism or not." (*International Socialist Review*, August, 1910.)

And a few months later the same gentleman observed:

"I am only one of the many *grains of sand* that help to make the soil upon which we expect to build the future civilization."

The two statements dovetail beautifully into each other: Keep the workers in ignorance of Socialism; build your house on grains of sand. Nothing could be truer nor more consistent—nor more deadly to the cause of working class emancipation. And although

---

this interview Mr. Thomas specifically disavowed the revolution. Unqualifiedly he said: "....We want no revolution...."

In the same interview Mr. Thomas said:

"Mr. Roosevelt is the best friend that capitalism has. It probably would have gone under before this had it not been for him. **He has adopted and adapted some Socialist ideas** [read "Socialist party ideas."—A.P.] **and used them as props for a shaky, falling structure. Without their support it would have already collapsed.**" (Bold face ours.)

Mr. Thomas is here literally arguing that **his** party, which he claims is Socialist, supplied the planks with which President Roosevelt shored up the capitalist system! He says, in effect, that if the Socialist party had not "built" those planks, and if Mr. Roosevelt had not "stolen" those planks, capitalism would have collapsed! Thus Mr. Thomas, self-styled Socialist, boasts that he saved capitalism, the destruction of which is the mission of Socialism!

Mr. Thomas may not have said the same thing in so many words, these are the precepts, this the example that he follows. At any rate, he and his fellow mourners at the wake of "bourgeois Socialism" have carried on consistently the traditional S.P. policy of lying about Socialism, thereby fully earning the plaudits and murmurs of approval tendered him from the camp of capitalism.

He was to be wined and dined in February, 1950, by "leading American figures," who included such stout defenders of capitalism as Harold Ickes, former Secretary of the Interior; Harry Woodburn Chase, Chancellor of New York University; Adolf A. Berle Jr., "New Dealer" par excellence; Robert David De Sola; Bishop Francis McConnell; Professor Reinhold Niebuhr, of Union Theological Seminary; Rev. Harry Emerson Fosdick, pastor emeritus of Rockefeller's church; Palmer Hoyt, publisher of the capitalist Denver *Post;* and a number of labor fakers and several renegade Marxists. A most interesting collection of the "cream" of capitalist society! Mr. Thomas must feel quite at home among them.[10]

---

[10] To this galaxy of capitalist stars should be added the Uultramontane politician, James A. Farley, pleader of the butcher Franco's cause, and the spawn of one of the most corrupt political machines in America. (The news reports of the banquet showed a picture of Thomas and Farley shaking hands, smirking and smiling, like reunited twins too long separated!) Mr. Farley, on this occasion, is reported as having said (New York "Times," February 5, 1950): "We would be better off with many more Americans like him." Such praise from an ultra-reactionary politician, admirer of the monster Franco, should have made Mr. Thomas wince, and apologize to his followers. Instead Mr. Thomas laughed loudly and most happily! Present also (or sending greetings) were the stone-age minded news commentator, H. V. Kaltenborn, the renegade Stalinist, Sidney

On the recent occasion of his 65th birthday he was again lauded by the chief plutocratic papers. The New York *Times* said that he had "won the respect of his countrymen," which is the paper's way of saying that he has won the approbation of the capitalist class as a whole. It acknowledges capitalism's debt to "bourgeois Socialism" by saying that "a good deal of the early [bogus] Socialist program has found its way. . . . into the law of the land." (That "Socialist" program consisted of the planks Thomas and his party made for the purpose of shoring up capitalism, and which he now complains the capitalist politicians stole from him!) The same paper, whose special pet he appears to be, said of him in 1948: "Mr. Thomas is about as far removed from the narrow, bitter and dogmatic spirit of Karl Marx as any man could be. . . ." Well, we can certainly all agree that Mr. Thomas is *far* removed from Marx, a fact upon which Marx is to be congratulated! The paper also referred to Mr. Thomas as "this sane, logical, humanitarian gentleman, this ex-preacher [who is] honestly trying to apply New

Hook, and sundry labor fakers and old-line capitalist politicians, including the capitalist pets, William Green, David Dubinsky and Dan Tobin—the last mentioned a particularly vicious and malicious slanderer of Socialism, against whom (or his union) Thomas even filed a libel suit, which he won! Indeed, a fine flock of birds of the same feather!

11 In his latest opus, "A Socialist's Faith," (page 28), just published (1951), Mr. Thomas took this fling at the Socialist Labor Party:

"In America, the Socialist Labor Party, oldest of Socialist parties, in the nineties had fallen under the vigorous leadership of Daniel De Leon, later to be praised by Lenin. For him the road to power demanded the organization of one big Marxist union—rather a federation of unions—of workers. Participation in elections was useful chiefly from an educational point of view. Once the workers were properly organized, they could

Testament ethics....," and so forth, *ad infinitum*. The New York *Times* is the most representative, the most influential, and by far the most consistent journalistic spokesman for capitalism and capitalist interests— indeed, it is in itself a huge capitalist enterprise. Hence, what this plutocratic organ considers "sane" and "logical" in a so-called Socialist candidate and Socialist program must necessarily constitute a rejection and repudiation of Socialism. And this is precisely the fact in the case of Mr. Thomas and his bankrupt party. [11]

---

demand and would receive a delivery of power into their hands. The threat of a general strike would be enough.

"Gene Debs never belonged to the Socialist Labor Party but was a leader in the Midwestern social-democratic group which in 1900 merged with the Socialists, who, under Morris Hillquit, split off from the Socialist Labor Party to form the present Socialist party."

True to his role of an apostle of "the machine for lying about Socialism," Mr. Thomas stupidly or brazenly misrepresents the principles and policies of the Socialist Labor Party. Outstanding among the lies he succeeded in packing into this brief statement is his claim that the S.L.P. advocates the general strike, when the truth is that the Party **condemns** the general strike and all its implications!

17

The S. P. Was
BOUND to Go Down

Now, at length, the end appears to have come. As reported recently in the WEEKLY PEOPLE, the N.E.C. of the bourgeois S.P. has decided to give up its pretense of being a party of Socialism, or a party of any kind.

Undoubtedly the leading S.P. politicians have long since realized that their party is hopelessly bankrupt. (Twelve years ago, referring to the New York City election of 1938, Mr. Thomas wrote in his little house organ, *The Call*: "I expected a very low....vote in New York. It was a little lower than I expected [!] ....We cannot continue primarily as a campaign organization, functioning at the polls in competition with the A.L.P.") Without Thomas as candidate and showman it is doubtful that it would have polled even the few thousand votes received in the 1948 election. The 1949 election (in which Thomas was not a candidate) demonstrated that as a party it is, in fact, non-existent.

With the pathetic and often ridiculous Norman Thomas running around shouting and gesticulating, and uttering all sorts of arrant nonsense in the name of Socialism, it has in truth been reduced to a one-man "party." In the 1949 New York City election the S.P. candidate for mayor received 3,396 votes, as against the 7,917 votes cast for the S.L.P. mayoralty candidate.

This pitiful number—pitiful for a party measuring its success solely by numbers—contrasts sharply with the 150,000 votes cast for Hillquit as mayoralty candidate in 1917 and the 250,000 cast for him for the same office in 1932!

The story of this decision is told in the sheetlet which the S.P. politicians humorously call their official organ, *The Call,* of November 18, 1949. The gist of the majority resolution (supported by Thomas and the leading politicians and officeholders) is conveyed in these two paragraphs:

(a) "We can no longer escape a basic re-evaluation of the Socialist party's electoral policy in relation to our success in spreading the message of Socialism, in building our own organization *and in paving the way for a new political alignment.* We must not allow our electoral policy to be decided by tradition [sic!], by drift or to go by default."

(b) "Candidates should not be nominated where a campaign would contribute, *or seem to our potential supporters to contribute,* to the triumph of reactionary candidates and policies opposed by *labor* and *liberal* forces. This does not imply, however, that the Socialist party, as such, should endorse candidates of either of the two major parties."

Let us try to translate this double- and triple-talk into plain English:

"The S.P. is bankrupt. We are compelled to admit it. We have utterly and completely failed, not alone as a party of Socialism, but even as the trail-blazer for a bourgeois-'liberal' party. We are sunk, we are *kaput* —let's not kid ourselves any longer.

"Where a 'liberal' capitalist candidate is running

111

for office, we must not place in nomination an opposing candidate. Let's help elect a 'good man.' To hell with principles—of which we never had any anyway.

"And look, boys, you better not endorse as a party [what party?] any candidates of either the Republican or Democratic party. That is, don't do it openly. There are ways, you know. Observe that innocent-sounding 'as such.' That means that individual S.P. members may endorse old party candidates—and there's where I, Norman Thomas, come in! It means also, by parity of reasoning, that individual S.P. members may accept endorsement by the old line politicians. And there's where I, Norman Thomas, come in again!

"Above all, we must have a party of the masses— no, we did *not* mean 'them asses.' (Although we have often said that the workers are too stupid to achieve their own emancipation. And they don't seem to want to be emancipated by us. Ingrates!)"

This decision to abandon the S.P. as a party with political pretensions is reinforced by the decision to seek unity with the aforesaid outfit calling itself the Social Democratic Federation, the so-called "right wing" of the S.P. when it "split" in 1936-1937. It is, in effect, if not in fact, a wing of the Liberal party, which runs top-ranking capitalist candidates on its ticket in New York State. [11]

And so, fifty years after the corrupt S.P. politicians and labor fakers split the Socialist movement in America, fifty years after they launched the bourgeois "Socialist" party as a bulwark for the corrupt and corrupting American Federation of Labor—hence, launched it

---

[11] See introduction.

as *a bulwark for capitalism*—the loathsome thing has reached its deserved, its *inevitable,* end. Yes, as De Leon said to me nearly forty years ago—emphasizing the point by pounding his fist on his desk—*"The S.P. is BOUND to go down."*

And so it was. The blasted hopes of sincere men, who fatuously believed in its Socialist claims and pretensions, lie like bleached bones on the road that stretches back to the date of the launching of the bourgeois "Socialist party."

We of the S.L.P. accept the passing of the S.P. with satisfaction, but not entirely joyfully. Those of us who have followed the course of the S.P. during the greater part of its existence know that the organization included thousands upon thousands of sincere men and women who hated capitalism, and who hailed Socialism as the emancipator of the working class and the redeemer of the human race.

But they were terribly confused, largely ignorant of the true meaning of Socialism, and misled by the catch-phrases of the slick lawyer-politicians and the pirate crew of privately owned papers catering to labor-fakerism. They became disillusioned, and, like most disillusioned persons, cynical. The S.P. politicians, past and present, have much to answer for at the bar of history. And not the least among their crimes is the debauching of the many thousands who came and went in the S.P. during the five decades of its existence. Most of these were honest when they entered, and if they left corrupted, the crime of corrupting them is to be charged against the most unscrupulous and unprincipled gang that ever plied the trade of social buccaneering in this country.

Through the years, the S.L.P. has held, and will continue to hold, the impregnable Marxist fort in this country. It will keep the proud banner of Marxism flying aloft—and it will never surrender, never cease its efforts to effect the organizing of the workers politically and industrially, to the end that wage slavery shall be no more, to the end of insuring a society dedicated to economic freedom, social equality and universal brotherhood founded on peace and plenty.

The present is a dark hour in the history of the world. Powerful forces are at work attempting to pull society back into the black night of industrial feudalism. They could succeed, but we say they shall not succeed! There lies in prospect before us a new shining era of human happiness and limitless progress. We do not, we *cannot,* doubt that we shall attain it. The S.L.P. will assuredly emerge out of the present contest with the crown of victory. In the words of De Leon: "The S.L.P. will beat its way to its goal athwart all gnashings of teeth!" For the S.L.P. principle is potent and sound to the core, our position unassailable. And the day cannot be far distant when the working class, chastened through the betrayals of misleaders, disenchanted through defeats by capitalism and its agents, and instructed by the science of Socialism, will marshall its battalions and, drilled in the army of industrial unionism, spearheaded by its own political party, march on the capitalist robberburg, razing it to the ground, rearing in its place the noble edifice of the Socialist Industrial Commonwealth. Soon or late (and rather *soon* than late) that army will be on the march. In the words of Jack London (who in his prime hailed the Socialist Labor Party in glowing terms) :

"The cry of this army is 'No Quarter.' We want all that you possess. We will be content with nothing less than all you possess. We want in our hands the reins of power and the destiny of mankind. HERE ARE OUR HANDS, THEY ARE STRONG HANDS. We are going to take your governments, your palaces and all your purpled ease away from you and in that day you shall work for your bread even as the peasant in the field and the starved and runty clerk in your metropolises. HERE ARE OUR HANDS. THEY ARE STRONG HANDS."

With unwavering faith in the working class and its capacity to achieve its emancipation through its own class efforts, the members of the Socialist Labor Party bend anew to the task, and hail with confidence the early coming of the dawn.

POSTLUDE

As this book is being prepared for the press, the latest spasms of the dying bourgeois S.P. have been reported. The National Executive Committee of the "Socialist party," in its February 17-18, 1951 meeting, repudiated in part its previous decision on the so-called electoral policy of the party. By a vote of 11 to 2 the N.E.C. decided to recommend for membership adoption a policy that would legalize what had long been a practice, namely, support of capitalist candidates where it was not considered "practicable to nominate Socialist [*sic!*] candidates." (See the *Socialist Call,* February 23, 1951.)

The minority charged the majority (which includes Norman Thomas and Darlington Hoopes) with trickery and double-dealing, without advancing any logical reasons for opposing the majority's decision. For once Norman Thomas & Co. were logical, if we disregard the hypocritical phrases with which they sought to cover their complete surrender to capitalist principles. Darlington Hoopes (S.P. candidate for Vice President in 1944) and Norman Thomas, in a statement prepared in behalf of the N.E.C., in which a "compromise" was offered, virtually acknowledged the bankruptcy of the S.P. Comparing the action of the February N.E.C. meeting with that of the previous one, the two gentlemen observed:

"Its chief difference is that it provides for some sort [!] of electoral activity by individual Socialists....*in the many areas* in which it is not at present practicable to nominate Socialist candidates."

In short, under this "plan" S.P. units may, if they desire, support pro-capitalist candidates, and this, the two precious fellows argue, would "restore morale and initiate new activity...."!

Speaking for the minority, S. H. Friedman of New York (one of the old S.P. wheelhorses and a veteran soap-boxer), charged that Thomas & Co. "had launched a campaign against the party decision (publicly supporting Democratic party candidates, and keeping the party in constant turmoil so that both electoral and other work was stymied) and had forced the Michigan comrades to arrive at a compromise...."

Mr. Friedman emphasizes that "the N.E.C. took no disciplinary action against these violators," because of its desire to "keep people in the party"; and that dissenters had been "bludgeoned by the violations of the other side [Thomas & Co.] into favoring the referendum NOW, in order to 'hold together the party' in the face of the actions by the other side [Thomas & Co.] splitting the party asunder."

Mr. Friedman adds that "when the Bridgeport party [Jasper McLevy & Co.] took a stand lining up electorally with reactionaries, the N.E.C. didn't at first condemn the action and then suggest that in order to restore morale and strengthen the party, every section of the party be permitted to do the same thing [i.e., "line up with reaction-aries"]." He concludes by demanding a "re-examination and re-appraisal of the party position by the party membership." Mr. Friedman is unrealistic—one does not "re-examine" and "re-appraise" a corpse. One secures a death certificate, and demands a decent burial.

The statement by the N.E.C. is a typical bourgeois Socialist product. Boasting that it supplied planks for Republican and Democratic party platforms, it whimpers feebly, "We have not failed"! And apparently without realizing the significance of their words, the authors of the statement explain:

"But the resources of American capitalism have met enough of the demands of the American people and of the immediate aims of the Socialist party, to keep them from turning to our ideal [!] of a cooperative commonwealth and a Socialist [!] America in a Socialist [!] world."

The Socialist Labor Party has ever contended that in the matter of palliatives and reforms, the capitalist class can outbid the reformer every time. What the fatuous S.P. reformers are actually saying here is that the S.L.P. was right in this contention. The "immediate demands" of the S.P. were matched again and again by the capitalist class, and then some! And the concessions were made by capitalism, not merely to cut the ground from under the S.P. politicians, but because the continued safety of capitalism demanded at least a degree of appeasement of the workers.

The result of the referendum on the proposed change in "electoral policy" was announced in the so-called official organ of the party, the *Socialist Call,* April 27, 1951. The action of the N.E.C. was approved overwhelmingly, by a vote of nearly two to one. The statement in the *Call* is extraordinarily brief, as if the editors were conscious of having betrayed the hopes of the many thousands who in the past had accepted the fraudulent S.P. as the genuine thing—the many thousands who spent fully of their time and substance on what they sincerely believed to be the noble cause of Socialism, despite the exposures of crooks

117

and swindlers in the party by De Leon and the S.L.P. generally. And this result of the final betrayal of its faithful supporters (ignorant of Socialism though they were) the current S.P. politicians announced in the issue of April 27, 1951—an issue ostensibly dedicated to May Day! As the WEEKLY PEOPLE (May 12, 1951) pointed out in commenting on the result of the referendum:

"The report took up a small part of [an inside] page devoted to paid greetings from members and organizations. One greeting read: 'Yours for the revolution.' Another read: 'This May Day let us never forget our goal. Nothing less than Socialism!' A third read: 'Socialism—the only solution for the world's present turmoil!' "

These sentiments were expressed in the face of the fact that the S.P. had just then finally abandoned even the pretense of fighting for the "revolution," for the "goal," for "Socialism"! A fitting mockery as commentary on the final bankruptcy of a party which in the name of Socialism has always mocked Socialism! A final lying pretense by a party that had justly earned the designation, "a machine for lying about Socialism"!

Whatever may happen to the individual members, the S.P. as such is "deader nor Caesar," as Artemus Ward would say. The local remnants (if any) will be indistinguishable from the splinter groups of capitalist reformism, for they will actually find themselves in the camp of capitalism where (in point of principles and practices) they had been right along. Any spasms this corpse may still experience will be indicative not of life, but of death.

Hic jacet!

Part Two

The

Renegade's Compulsion:

A Study
In Mendacity and Perversion

By Arnold Petersen

The tactical position of the Socialist Labor Party on the political field, since the convention of 1900, has been correct. This I have never heard disputed by members of the Socialist party whose opinions carry weight among the thoughtful and well-informed.

—*FRANK BOHN,*
"International Socialist Review," June 1908.

1

"Still violent, whatever cause he took,
But most against the party he forsook;
For renegadoes, who ne'er turn by halves,
Are bound in conscience to be double knaves."

(John Dryden)

The "Double Knaves"

It is a generally recognized fact that those who desert a faith often become the most virulent haters of that faith. Unless they find their balance in a principle and a cause that not only supply a substitute for the lost faith, but also endow them with a philosophy that enables them to appraise all faiths in their proper setting and perspective, they find themselves under the compulsion of assailing their erstwhile faith by any means, fair or foul—usually foul. The psychoanalysts have an explanation for this phenomenon, but let us skip that.

What is true in the case of deserters from a religious faith is even more so in the case of deserters from a political creed, and it is universally true of renegades from Marxian Socialism, or (to apply a necessary qualification) what the renegades conceive to be Socialism. The list of those who have deserted the movement of working class emancipation (whatever may have been their understanding of the basic principles of that movement) is a long one, and it stretches back almost to the beginning of the Socialist movement. Such desertions, however, have been most numerous since

World War I. However fundamentally wrong one must consider such movements as the "Socialist party" or the "Communist party," it cannot be denied that most of those who have joined them have been sincere in their Socialist professions—again, regardless of their understanding of Socialist principles, or their lack of it. But many have also joined for the most sordid reasons —the desire to make soft berths for themselves, or the compulsion to satisfy egotistical cravings (to be featured as writers, orators or "leaders," etc.), and in general to occupy the spotlight and to revel in the applause of the multitude. It would be difficult to say which of these groups labored under the greater compulsion—those who were motivated by a craving for the spotlight, the thirst for power; or those who simply saw an opportunity for an easy living in comfort or affluence. In either case principles (if they entered into consideration at all) were of secondary importance.

To repeat, the list of those who have deserted the Socialist movement (or what passed as such) is a long one—and so is the list of those who have deserted the so-called Communist cause, most of whom no doubt had convinced themselves that they were, or had been, sincere Socialists. Going back only to World War I, the list would include such onetime professed Socialists as Walter Lippmann, Charles E. Russell, William J. Ghent, John Spargo, William English Walling, J. Graham Phelps Stokes, A. M. Simons, Robert Hunter, "Professor" Will Durant, Sidney Hillman, Joseph Schlossberg, Benjamin Stolberg (now a Dubinsky pensioner), Jacob Potofsky, Daniel W. Hoan, Andrew Biemiller, the two Bohns (Frank and William), and many others.

The list of those who have deserted the "Communist" (later Stalinist) party (as members or fellow travelers) is probably an even longer one. It includes such well-known, or well-remembered, figures as Benjamin Gitlow, Jay Lovestone (Jacob Liebstein), Eugene Lyons, Granville Hicks, William H. Chamberlin, John Chamberlain (both the latter now holding editorial jobs with ultra-plutocratic journals), Waldo Frank, Whittaker Chambers, Edmund Wilson, Max Eastman, Bertram D. Wolfe, Sidney Hook, Sherwood Anderson, Malcolm Cowley, Clifton Fadiman, Samuel Putnam, John Dos Passos,etc. To descend to an even lower level, this list should also include Louis C. Fraina (now "Professor Lewis Corey"), "Professor" Louis Budenz and William Z. Foster. (Some may object to the inclusion of Foster, since he is the top fuehrer of the current Stalinist outfit. However, since Foster ["Zig-Zag"] is several times a renegade, he properly belongs here.)

2

Out–Heroding Herod

With few, if any, exceptions those named above have renounced and/or denounced Socialism since their apostasy, either in direct terms, or by repudiating (with or without sneers) Marx and Marxian Socialism. There have been differences in the degree of the virulence with which they have done so, and some have sought to justify their apostasy while others have attempted to conceal their "indiscreet" past in a cloud of unrestrained vilification and base slanders and lies. But with hardly an exception all have eagerly sought to certify to their present faith in "democracy" (meaning, of course, capitalist democracy) and, lest they be suspected of remaining heretics, they have been among the loudest in denouncing and repudiating those who did not join them in their apostasy.

It is not difficult to understand why they have thus tried to "out-Herod Herod." For one thing they are frightened—fear rules them as completely as ignorance and/or folly ruled them during their "revolutionary" period. For another thing, because of their "shady" past they must forever offer assurances to their capitalist masters and patrons that they are really and truly cured of their "folly"—that they are now thoroughly to be trusted, even more so than those plutocratic servitors who never passed through the purgatory of "radical leftism." Finally, many of them are troubled by their consciences. Not all of them renounced Social-

ism for sordid reasons, or because of a sudden recon-
version to faith in capitalist principles. Some, no doubt,
secretly admit to themselves that the dream of their
"nonage" (to use a Shavian phrase) may not after all
have been wholly utopian. Some, no doubt, still feel
(or fear) that those whom they deserted or betrayed
may eventually come out on top, and the thought of
such a possibility may well chill the marrow of the
boldest renegade's bones! As Shakespeare reminded
us, "Conscience does make cowards of us all."!

It is not our intention here to go into the case histories of all the renegades listed above. That, if worth
the trouble, may be done on another occasion. But
among the assorted characters listed there is one who
more than any other deserves to be "vivisected" at this
time, partly because he is of the more contemptible
sort, and partly because he has repeatedly slandered
and vilified the Socialist Labor Party and Daniel De
Leon. This particular renegade is one William E.
Bohn, onetime "blood-and-thunder 'revolutionist,'"
and currently editor of the now thoroughly respectable
bourgeois liberal weekly, the *New Leader*. Here, in
his special column, he ruminates on things past and
present, mostly past. For even when he discusses current topics, his comments are for the most part in terms
of the dead past.

Nothing is too reactionary to merit his approval.
In characteristic renegade fashion he has truckled to
Ultramontanism, and lauded the clerical politicians as
libertarians. In the *New Leader,* July 30, 1949, for
example, he wrote (or approved) an editorial which
(though purporting to reprove the uncivilized Ultra-
montane chief Spellman for his spat with Mrs. Roose-

velt) cleared the hierarchy of the well-founded charge that it is "reactionary and itself practices intolerance, authoritarianism and thought control." (This legitimate charge was referred to as a "Communist charge"!) And in the same editorial he vowed that "a great army of American libertarians stands ready to defend those [hierarchal] rights unto death."

He has reproved the capitalist-manned Congress for its failure to enact, or its delay in enacting, peacetime conscription and universal military training! He has hailed the capitalist system in such words as these: "Actually, there has never been a more flexible economic system [capitalism] than ours. . . . It works. It works very well." (*New Leader,* July 9, 1949.) Indignantly he has rejected the charge (made in the Vatican organ, *Osservatore Romano* !!) that capitalism is "a system that seeks to concentrate the major part of the goods in the hands of a few men."!! (How servile *can* a "Social Democratic-Liberal" defender of capitalism get?)[1] And angrily this plutocratic servitor

---

[1] Perhaps an even lower depth as a truckling renegade was achieved by "Dr." Bohn in his column in the "New Leader" of October 14, 1950. Under the title "Teaching Congress the Facts of Life" he undertakes to instruct the capitalist Congress in the art of dealing with "subversives," specifically the American Stalinists. He is generally critical of the so-called McCarran Act—not because it is reactionary and unconstitutional, but because it is "inadequate," that is, it does not go far enough! However, he hails with satisfaction one of the most Nazi-like provisions of this infamous act. To quote him:

"There is only one part of the bill which seems to me calculated to serve this purpose [i.e., "to decrease the number of Communists," etc.] That is the section which provides that, in case of war, Communists are to be rounded up and segregated. That is a plain military measure. **No one can complain that it contravenes anyone's civil rights.**" (Emphasis mine.)

No one, that is, except American citizens who (foolishly and regrettably) have chosen to be Communists! What this re-added: "It is about time we began to let Europeans know what really goes on here."

In a sneering article he bracketed the Socialist Labor Party with the Socialist party and a Communist splinter group, alleging that it represents "ideas which belong to our political past." Exempting his pal, Norman Thomas, from this classification (and differentiating him from the Socialist party, which, he said, "has practically disappeared"), he extolled this ex-reverend "as a national preacher and teacher, a chaplain to the entire American people"—"people" in this context meaning capitalist America!

Finally, in an article in the *New Leader*, February 18, 1950, he ruminated on his past and current capitalist allegiances, "as one who began life as an Ohio Republican in the age of McKinley and Hanna....," and, "as a supporter of President Truman and his Fair Deal....," showing that he has tried a bit of everything in the line of capitalist politics. But what he omits in this chronology is of vastly greater interest than the things he includes. For between his McKinley and Truman allegiances there lies a chapter about which he never "says a mum'lin' word."! And this brings us to the special occasion for this brief "case history" of a renegade of the most contemptible kind.

---

pulsive renegade is saying is that a Communist (though an American citizen) has no civil rights. "Dr." Bohn here out-Rankins Rankin! We hold no brief for the stupid American Stalinists, but to argue that an American citizen who is a Communist has no constitutional rights, is to propose to ditch the Bill of Rights, and to hold in contempt all that the revolutionary fathers (specifically Jefferson) fought for. Bohn's reactionary stand certifies him as a 100 per cent subversive. By all that is proper and fitting he should be shipped off to Stalinist Russia! At any rate, he should not find it difficult to accept the rules and practices of Stalinist despotism.

3

The Mendacious Bohn

As mentioned before, "Dr." Bohn never fails to revile or lie about the S.L.P., and especially about De Leon, when an opportunity for doing so presents itself. His latest effort in this regard was part of a eulogy he paid that other fugitive from a supposed Socialist past, the old charlatan and humbug who so often out-Hearsted Hearst, Abraham Cahan, who recently celebrated his 90th birthday. He hailed Cahan as a "fighting American moralist [!] in the tradition of Teddy Roosevelt, Wilson, Gompers [!] and Debs [!]." Continuing, he rhapsodized: "But all of us owe an infinite debt to this man: for the example of his first 90 years is vibrant proof that good men and fighters are not lost here [!], that the strength and purity [!] of a battling spirit can move and uplift millions, and that the American dream can be realized by those who believe in it." !!

Having introduced his hero, the pure angel Abe Cahan, he must (like a good stage manager) also introduce his villain, who turns out to be none other than Mephisto himself, Daniel De Leon! And so he contrived the following piece of infamous villainy:

"Few alive today remember that we had Communism in America in 1890 and 1900. *Its leader was a man named Daniel De Leon.* From the moment Abraham Cahan took up his pen down on the East Side, he fought this early brand of Communism. I recall vividly [!] that when De Leon tried to infiltrate the labor movement—*just like the followers of Mr. Foster to-day*—he used every sort of dirty slander to destroy this young man from Vilna. Cahan, from the moment he stepped off the gangplank, *was too good an American to be taken in."!!* (Italics ours.)

To appreciate fully the enormity of this piece of brazen journalistic scoundrelism, one must know the past career of this man who so unscrupulously and mendaciously slanders the illustrious social scientist who, more than anyone else in the American labor movement, fought against the things now associated with the unspeakable Foster and his Stalinist co-conspirators.

To place Bohn's eulogy of Abe Cahan in its proper setting, let us first introduce a Cahan character witness —a man who knew the "East Side Hearst" inside out and who at one time did not hesitate to speak out against him and the evil he represented, though our witness's subsequent apostasy has now placed him in the Cahan-Bohn section of the capitalist camp. He is Joseph Schlossberg, onetime editor of a Jewish S.L.P. organ, who later betrayed the Party and became a loyal "labor lieutenant" of capitalism, serving as General Secretary of the Amalgamated Clothing Workers of America for about a quarter of a century, and right-hand man of the shrewd labor politician, Sidney Hillman, who in turn was one of Franklin D. Roosevelt's trusted errand boys. ("Clear it with Sidney!") This is what Mr. Schlossberg said of Abe Cahan and his yellow sheet in an article he wrote in the *Daily People,* July 3, 1910:

"The *Vorwaerts* [*Forward*] is the Yiddish yellow journal par excellence. There is nothing yellower in the Jewish language in any part of the world. It is yellow in its 'Socialist' writings. Among its 'Socialist' editorials the reader will find such 'revolutionary' instructive matter as congratulations to President [Theodore] Roosevelt upon the marriage of his daughter. In other departments the most obscene and morally disgusting points are taken out from a 'juicy' story, are magnified and illustrated, and printed under a suggestive headline. It consistently excludes from its columns anything that is really instructive and enlightening. It has reduced its own writers to mere mechanical quill-pushers without will or individuality. Some time ago, it locked out a part of its editorial staff, and the secret then leaked out—through its own columns—that the editorial department of the *Vorwaerts* is a literary sweatshop with a 'foreman' as slave-driver at its head.

"On the whole the *Vorwaerts* is a tremendous engine of demoralization for the Jewish workingmen.

"It prints with impunity want ads for scabs for firms whose men are on strike, often in the same issue that contains reports of the very strikes in its backdoor department of labor news. It must be remembered that the most conspicuous parts of the paper are devoted to sensations and scandals. Socialist and labor news items are relegated to the most obscure end of the paper, printed in a modest and unpretentious manner. At the time the S.L.P. press sounded its strongest bugle to announce the kidnapping of Moyer, Haywood and Pettibone, the *Vorwaerts* devoted to it a few lines in a place where it was overlooked by most of its readers, printed under a small headline. If the wife of a multi-millionaire runs away with her husband's lackey,

it is sure to be reported on the front page with a three-
or four-column headline, accompanied by the pictures
of the husband, wife, lover, auto, lap puppets, and even
the bedrooms. But such trifles as the kidnapping of
labor leaders—who cares for them! But as soon as the
capitalist press took up the Moyer-Haywood affair
strongly, as soon as the *Vorwaerts* realized that there
was no less sensation in that than in a scandalous elope-
ment or divorce, the Western labor fight was dignified
by being placed alongside of the seductions, divorces
and elopements, that is, in the most important part of
the paper.

"The *Vorwaerts* is in a position to boost or break—
though not to win—any strike. The labor unions dare
not, therefore, raise their voice against any rascality or
treachery committed by that paper against the interests of labor. Nor would any labor leader permit his
union to do any such thing, for that would mean his
ruin."

4

Bohn's "Radical" Past

So much for "Dr." Bohn's hero. Now let us see who is the real villain in the piece. How or when William E. Bohn first entered what passed for the Socialist and labor movement in this country is a bit obscure. The first time his name came to the notice of the present writer was in 1908. In the April, 1908, issue of the *International Socialist Review* his name appeared (apparently for the first time) under the department head, "International Notes," and it continued to appear there regularly for at least five or six years. The *International Socialist Review* was the monthly magazine (published by Chas. H. Kerr & Co.) that represented the "left wing" in the "Socialist party." Its editors and contributors constituted a motley crew, ranging all the way from the "pure and simple" politicians of the Hillquit-Berger type to the Haywood roughneck (later "pure and simple" physical forcist) type, with Debs occupying a place somewhere in between.

When, in 1905, the Industrial Workers of the World (then pro-political action) was founded, it was acclaimed mildly, but with occasional dissident notes, by such editors of the *Review* as A. M. Simons and Max Hayes.

The dominant element on the *Review*, however, seemingly took an increasing interest in the new revolutionary labor union, and among those who were particularly vociferous on its behalf (especially after the

1908 anarchist coup) were William E. Bohn and his brother, Frank Bohn. The latter, ex-National Secretary of the Socialist Labor Party, had deserted the S.L.P. for the S.P., and there attached himself to the "left wing."

Frank Bohn (about 1910 or 1911) co-authored with William D. Haywood a pamphlet entitled "Industrial Socialism." Despite its obvious defects it was not without some merit. Its espousal of industrial unionism, supposedly a point in its favor, was actually its fatal weakness, for by this time the "industrial unionism" hailed by the Bohns and Haywood was physically represented by the anti-political, or anarcho-syndicalist I.W.W.

When the 1908 convention of the Industrial Workers of the World (through rump proceedings) struck the political clause from the preamble of the I.W.W. as originally founded in 1905, the *International Socialist Review* and its editors, willy-nilly, became committed to the anarcho-syndicalist program of the emasculated I.W.W., no matter how much they individually might have protested their belief in political action.

Men are judged by their acts, not by their words alone. The anarcho-syndicalist element grew in favor with the publisher and editors of the *International Socialist Review,* and this fact was increasingly reflected in the articles and letters published in the magazine. Eventually the policy of the magazine collided violently with the official policy of the S.P., and the *Review's* attacks on the S.P. politicians increased in virulence. The Bohns were among the loudest in these "r-r-revolutionary" denunciations of the politicians, and eventually the break came, but that is another story.

Month after month William E. Bohn, in his special department and in articles he wrote for the magazine, fulminated against the "reformers" in the S.P., against the Catholic Church, and against the capitalist government and capitalism generally. *His attitude and language were then scarcely distinguishable from the attitude and language of William Z. Foster and the anarcho-Communists (Stalinists) of today.* Take, for example, an article he wrote for the September, 1909, issue of the *International Socialist Review* under the title, "Reformer and Revolutionist." In this article he discusses the policies and ideas of the two wings in the S.P., the wing of the "reformers" (the Hillquit-Berger element) and that of the "revolutionists" (the Haywood-Bohn-Debs element). For William E. Bohn was, of course, a fiery "revolutionist"! Here is a sample of his "revolutionary" mouthings:

"Is not your reformer always telling us that all we need is a majority of votes? Does he not calm our minds with the assurance that we can get 'Socialism' little by little; pass now one law, now another, take over first this industry, then that, under government control? And your revolutionist [Me—Bohn!]—is he not always talking of the class struggle, strikes and lockouts? Does he not represent the advent of Socialism AS THE RESULT OF A BETTER [BITTER?] PHYSICAL FIGHT, a fight quite beyond control of the State?"

(Contrast this with the Bohn of today and his valiant defense of "our economic system"—his contempt for revolutionary policies and principles!)

Posing the question *pro* and *con,* our "revolutionary" hero arrived at the "right" answer "as to what is the best line of tactics for those who wish to overthrow the existing society" (his words), and he proclaimed it proudly:

"How and where does the capitalist class use its industrial power—i.e., where does it bring its power to bear effectively on the masses of the people? Obviously in factory or mine or on the transportation line. *The forces of government are only subsidiary to powers exercised directly in these places.* Our question is answered; the working class, too, must learn to use its power in factory and mine and on transportation line. Then, whenever there is a strike or lockout or the drawing up of an agreement, *the real struggle for the REVOLUTION is on."* (Emphases ours.)

And the Bohn who is now a "loyal" defender of "our way of life," and a dreamer of the American capitalist dream, concluded his "r-r-r-revolutionary" invocation as follows, to wit:

"I say this, not because it is necessary to get into the confidence of the workingman, to interest him in our party, but because working class organization *is the only means to a revolution.* Our present labor movement is pitifully inadequate. [Tell that to your present patrons, William Green, Philip Murray, David Dubinsky and Walter Reuther, "Doc" Bohn!]. What we need is a great, solid organization of workers, class-conscience [sic], industrially organized, *fighting capitalism at every step,* and so, growing as capitalism grows, steadily evolving into the *industrial commonwealth."* (Italics ours.)

Ah, dreams of our youth—our "American dream"!!

Throughout his comments on "international events," this veiled anarcho-syndicalist (professing belief in political action, yet deriding it on many occasions) uttered sentiments so shocking that they would surely give the present aged William E. Bohn indigestion so acute as to result in heart failure! A pamphlet could be filled with samples of such "shocking" quotations, and if one were so constituted one might derive a certain sadistic pleasure from doing just that. But, in addition to humanitarian feelings, considerations of time and space, imposing the necessity of brevity, forbid such indulgence. And so only a few additional samples will be recorded here.

5

Bohn's "Stalinist" Past

In view of "Dr." Bohn's present defense of "our economic system," his "patriotism" and his denunciations of "irresponsible strikes" that hurt "our national interest," the following tidbit from his "Notes" in the August, 1908, issue of the *International Socialist Review* is revealing. Commenting on the "murder at Draveil [France] of defenseless strikers by the *gendarmerie*," he wrote:

"For example, it was suggested that the miners might prevent war by refusing to supply war vessels with coal. *Such a feeling of classconsciousness and social responsibility* [sic] *as is shown in this suggestion is surely significant of a real proletarian awakening.*"

Commenting approvingly on action taken in France "toward bridging the gulf between Socialism and syndicalism," he said (*Ibid*, January, 1909):

"One who remembers how but a few years ago the Socialists were torn by dissensions, how one group was sitting in parliament cheek by jowl with the radicals [!], how workingmen had lost faith in politicians [!], *cannot but congratulate our French comrades on the progress they have made.* Their party stands today united for *revolutionary Socialism"!*

When the Russian Revolution took place (long before the Stalinist counter-revolution), Bohn denounced Lenin and his co-workers as enemies of (capitalist) "democracy." (By that time he had returned to the capitalist fold.) In the *International Socialist Review* (April, 1909) he wrote on the situation in Russia, under the subhead: "What Has Become of the Revolution?" He commented: "The labor movement must in the nature of things be revolutionary. As soon as it gets under way [in Russia] *we shall have a real revolution,* with its roots deep in the needs and determination of the majority."

Commenting (in the *International Socialist Review,* May, 1909) on the Italian elections, this present apologist for Ultramontanism lauded the sharpening of the issue between the Socialists and the clerical politicians in these words:

"Thus the fight between the Socialists and the Roman Church becomes clearer cut. *This, of course, is a highly desirable state of affairs.*"

And in the same connection he hailed with joy the reconciliation between the Socialists and the anarchists, adding:

"Nowhere are the workers more steadily gravitating toward Socialism than in Italy."!!

While on the subject of "Dr." Bohn's friends, the Ultramontanes, it is interesting to note his comments on the murder of Francisco Ferrer by the Spanish clericalist regime. He wrote (in the *International Socialist Review,* November, 1909):

"For a long time the clerical powers of Spain had been seeking his life. In 1907 he eluded their bloody grasp. [!] The riots of last July gave them another opportunity. The Archbishop of Barcelona [a 1909 Spanish Spellman] sent to Senor Maura a protest against the uprising and the individuals who are responsible therefor; that is to say, the partisans of godless schools [Ferrer's], the radical press, and the anarchist groups. Then it was suddenly discovered that the founder of the Modern Schools [Ferrer] was the chief aider and abettor of the riots . . . . he was an enemy of the Church; so he was sentenced to death . . . Religious bigotry had found another victim: what of that? . . . . The news of this latest martyrdom acted like the acid in the retort: it separated the powers of light [Socialism] from those of darkness [the Roman Catholic Church] . . . . No better evidence could there be to show which are the forces of progress, the representatives of enlightenment."

A month later he commented on "Ferrer's murderer's [i.e., the Spanish Catholic Church's] attempt to blacken his memory," asserting: "Roman Catholic journals have published certain palpable fabrications about his trial . . . ."

Bohn's "libertarian" friend, Cardinal Spellman, would not have liked such "bigoted" talk at all. Beware, Doc Bohn!

Remembering Bohn's praise of Sam Gompers as "a fighting American moralist" (bracketed as such with "spiked police club" Teddy Roosevelt!), we note with interest his comments on Gompers' European trip in 1909 (*International Socialist Review,* October, 1909):

"The backwardness of the American labor movement was never more dramatically exhibited than in Mr. Samuel Gompers' recent European tour."

Having thus identified his present-day hero as a reactionary, as a tool of capitalist interests, Bohn thereupon reported on the reception Gompers was given by the European labor leaders (who were anything but revolutionary themselves!), approvingly quoting Karl

Kautsky as saying "that he [Gompers] is a good deal of a demagogue."! And he concluded his report by saying that "everywhere, then, Mr. Gompers was met by leaders more advanced than he, most of them Socialists."

6

Bohn's "War" On Reformism

Throughout his "Notes," Bohn indulged in revolutionary phrase-mongering, invariably falling into the *patois* of the anarchists and the anti-political syndicalists. In October, 1909, he declaimed: "What counts is the revolutionary strike." And for good measure he added: "It takes classconscious thinking and class-conscious organization [i.e., the anarcho-syndicalist I.W.W.] together to put labor in the position of power which of right belongs to it." (Hush! Don't let Messrs. Green, Murray and Dubinsky get wind of that, Doc Bohn!)

Again, writing on Argentina's labor movement (*International Socialist Review,* September, 1910), Bohn joyously reported that in Argentina "the general strike is being kept up, and in some industries is fairly effective." And of the same country he wrote: "All of these periodicals are filled with the spirit of classconscious revolution."

Bohn's conception of industrial unionism is illustrated in the praise he bestowed on the notorious British anarcho-syndicalist, Tom Mann, later a convert to, and a hero of, Stalinism. Hailing Tom Mann's arrival in Great Britain following his Australian tour, he jubilantly reported:

"From the very first remarks with which he [Mann] hailed the comrades who greeted him at the dock to

his latest writings and speeches, everything he has said
has teemed with the spirit of working class solidarity."

Bohn quoted a British reviewer of Mann's then
recent pamphlet, "Industrial Syndicalist" (a characteristic anarcho-syndicalist title), as saying that "Mr.
Mann is so reasonable an industrial unionist that he is
hardly an industrial unionist at all."!! At which "most
unkindest cut" Bohn waxed wroth, commenting that
thus to treat his hero "is hardly graceful and gra-
cious." Dear me!

With obvious sympathy Bohn reported an interview he had in 1910 with Karl Liebknecht, who later
was murdered by the forerunners of Doc Bohn's present-day friends and associates, the labor fakers and
Social Democrats of post-World War I Germany. In
the *International Socialist Review* (November, 1910)
we find Bohn writing:

"He [Liebknecht] had shown that industrial Europe and industrial America are but parts of the same
great world development. *He had proved that we are
all fighting the same masters.* And with tremendous
power [!] he had called on the toilers of the new
world to unite themselves as one man to those of the
old. So I felt a bit ashamed [!] of myself when I ap-
proached with commonplace questions about German
tactics and the state of the German movement. But
a moment's talk showed me that to this man there is
nought of the commonplace in anything that has to do
with the struggle of the world's workers."

Today William E. Bohn would slander his 1910
hero in the same terms, and largely for the same reasons, that he has employed and advanced against
America's great working class educator and champion,
Daniel De Leon.

Today Doc Bohn is an admirer of British "Socialism," that monstrous caricature and perversion of genuine Marxian Socialism. Not so in his "r-r-revolutionary" period. Then he railed at the Labor politicians, denouncing them as traitors and what not. In the *International Socialist Review* of March, 1910, he wrote: "The Labor party has sold its birthright for the mere chance of securing a mess of pottage." And in February, 1911, he wrote:

"The Labor party of Australia bears no resemblance to the Labor party of England. *It is full of classconscious determined workers.* [!] Its press fights consistently and intelligently for the working class. The party objective, which is Socialism, is never lost sight of."

We are not here concerned with this grotesque and false estimate of the Australian Labor party. The point here is that Bohn, by contrasting the British Labor party with its Australian counterpart, condemns the former as a reactionary, anti-Socialist outfit. But today that same British Labor party (though even more reactionary than in 1910) is saluted by him in terms of praise as unrestrained as were his condemnatory remarks in 1910! Oh, yes—the world do move, even though (as in the case of Bohn himself) it does so sometimes in crablike fashion!

7

Bohn on the Class Struggle And War

And now just a few samples of Doc Bohn's general "revolutionary phrase-mongering" (as he would designate such denunciatory language today!) :

"The capitalist world knows where the vital struggle of modern society is taking place. It talks a good deal about politics and war [as Bohn does today], but it is the conflict between employers and employed that makes the cold shivers run up and down its spinal cord. The capitalist may well be proud of his classconsciousness. He has few illusions about the class struggle." (*International Socialist Review,* June, 1909.)

And this:

"One might think that the lords of industry themselves would recognize the economic value of this proposal [relief for the needy]. But of course they will not. . . . Real relief of the poor is not on the capitalist program." (*Ibid.,* September, 1909.)

And:

"As a matter of principle Socialists have regarded the endorsement of a bourgeois budget as *the surrender of power to the hand of an enemy.*" (*Ibid.,* January, 1910.)

And this:

"We in this country have few illusions about bourgeois republicanism. We know very well how a great revolutionary uprising can be turned to advantage by the powers of capitalism. We know how the revolutionary ideals are twisted and turned into their opposites once capitalism has got fully under way." (*Ibid.*, December, 1910.)

Also this gem:

"Our political governments are controlled by the capitalist class, and their energies are devoted to maintaining the rule of that class." (*Ibid.*, July, 1911.)

Bohn was an ardent supporter of the second world war—a war that more than any previous one proved itself to be a war of conflicting capitalist economic interests, hence a war born of the capitalist-imperialist profit system. In that war Bohn was a swivel-chair fellow combatant of Joseph Stalin no less than of John D. Rockefeller Jr. World War II differed from World War I only in degree—it was by many more degrees a war of capitalism than the latter.

In the *International Socialist Review* of October, 1914, Bohn wrote:

"It is the war of big business. This was explained in detail last month, *but it must be insisted on always.*"

Always? Well, for a little while anyhow! For within a short time Doc Bohn sang lustily in the "patriotic" chorus, joined by his loving kinsman, Frankie Bohn! Yet, of the fruits of that war, and the pillars of society who supported it, he wrote in the same article:

"When capitalist judge or legislature poses before us as defender of property we can point to Louvain. There is the perfect work of our money-getting system. Nothing is sacred before it. *We knew it had no regard for life.* Now we know it has no regard for science, for art, for craftsmanship, for property."

Well, there it is, laddies. Ol' Bill Bohn hath said it!

8

Bohn on Renegades

There are many more such "revolutionary" and "irresponsible" statements by the currently ultra-respectable upholder of "our economic system," "Dr." William E. Bohn. They measure, not merely the distance traveled by him since he made them, but also the mental and intellectual depravity of the renegade who can condemn in sneering and contemptuous terms the high ideals that he professed, the principles and the cause that he espoused, at an earlier period in his life. No honest, no decent man could do that. Renegades can, and do.

In his own words Bohn has pronounced the judgment and expressed the contempt due the cowardly and hypocritical renegade. Enrico Ferri was at one time a prominent Italian Socialist, a leading member of the Italian party during the first decade of this century, a man of some learning—in short, an "intellectual." Like the earlier Bohn he had spouted "r-r-revolutionary" phrases, and (like the Bohn of today) he presently "saw the light." As Bohn himself reported the incident (*International Socialist Review,* February, 1910):

"About the middle of the month the startling announcement came that Enrico Ferri, whom we knew less than ten years ago as the inspired leader of the revolutionary forces, had broken away from his parliamentary group and declared his willingness to support the government."

Bohn concluded his comments by saying: "It seems that the name of Enrico Ferri must be added to those of Clemenceau, Millerand, Briand and the host of others who have deserted the cause for the sake of 'something now'—and that something for themselves."

How do *you* like your "something now," Doc Bohn? And does it feel good to be in the company of those whom you yourself have labeled traitors, renegades, and deserters of the cause? Foolish question, isn't it? For you were, of course, as sincere, honest and truthful then as you are now, and are as much to be trusted by your present patrons as you were by your "comrades" of your manhood (?) years! Or was Cicero right when he said that "no wise man ever thought that a traitor should be trusted"?

As mentioned before, Bohn cited Aristide Briand (former anarchist, professed Socialist, and later reactionary Premier of France) as one who betrayed his class for "something now." In his column in the December, 1910, issue of the *International Socialist Review*, Bohn told a story about Briand that pointed up the treason of that wretched character. This story also sheds a flood of light on Bohn's own treachery. Reporting on the great railroad strike that took place in France at the time, he showed how well Briand served his capitalist masters, and how justified were their faith and confidence in this working class traitor. Under the subhead, "Class Against Class," Bohn sounded off dramatically, bombastically:

"Again the Gallic cock has crowed. Again the working class of the world has taken new courage.

Again international capitalism has suffered a spasm of terror."!!

The great strike was of short duration. It was crushed by the renegade Briand, who caused the arrest of the strike leaders and drafted into the army all strikers who were subject to military duty. Twenty officials of the railway unions were ordered arrested. But let Doc Bohn tell the story:

"The twenty men involved let it be known that they would assemble in the editorial room of *l'Humanite,* the Socialist daily, and there await the officers of the law. On the wall of that room hangs a drawing representing a company of soldiers beating down a crowd of proletarians, men, women and children. Under the drawing is an excerpt from an address delivered by ["Socialist"] Aristide Briand in 1899: 'Fellow workers, take up scythes, clubs, pikes! On to the fight against your enemies, the exploiters of the people! In the midst of the conflict I will be with you.' When the minions of the law came to execute the commands of this Briand they took one of the representatives of the working class from the very chair in which Briand himself, as editorial writer on *l'Humanite,* had toiled for working class supremacy. On the table lay the very pen with which he had written his impassioned appeals."

Was this embarrassing to Briand? One might suppose so, but the old scoundrel gave no outward indication of it. Nor will Doc Bohn manifest any embarrassment when confronted with his own past record— a record that parallels that of Briand and every other renegade from earliest times down to our own. Only a few traitors suffer death for their treason, but every traitor (if he was originally sincere) suffers death within himself, and as added punishment he must suffer the humiliation of having to live with himself.

The moral of the Briand story, told by Bohn, is of course plain. In principle there is no difference between the treason of Briand and that of Bohn. In condemning the Briand treason, he has condemned his own subsequent treachery.

9

Bohn's Intellectual Equipment Consists Of Lies

In the light of Bohn's revealed record, let us now advert to his lying statement about Daniel De Leon: "Few alive today remember that we had Communism in America in 1890 and 1900. Its leader was a man named Daniel De Leon."

The enormity of this corrupt falsehood now stands fully revealed. Daniel De Leon was a Marxian Socialist. Bohn knows that. He knows also that De Leon fought relentlessly against the corruption in the Socialist movement, and against every advocate of pure and simple physical force, against preachers and practitioners of sabotage, against conspiracies and conspirators, whether underground or otherwise. De Leon fought tirelessly against the very tactics now associated with the names of W. Z. Foster and Stalinism—tactics that were substantially the same as those employed by the anarcho-syndicalist I.W.W., *with which William E. Bohn was associated, and whose program and principles he espoused.*

Bohn knows also that "Communism" (as originally understood) was synonymous with Marxian Socialism, the term having subsequently been stolen by the Stalinist counter-revolutionists, and corrupted by them into the very antithesis of Marxism. Now, if Bohn called

De Leon a "Communist" because this great social scientist was a Marxian Socialist, then by the same token Bohn was also a "Communist," for he claimed to be a Marxian Socialist! We have seen, however, that Bohn was, in fact, much closer to being what would now be called a Stalinist "Communist" than a Marxian Socialist. His whole "revolutionary" career, his social "philosophy," his language, his associates—all justify placing him in the category of anarcho-syndicalism, the "Stalinism" of forty and more years ago. And in one more respect he shares the characteristics of present-day Stalinism (and Hitlerism): his use of "The Big Lie" technique. For of such is his infamously false reference to Daniel De Leon.

Equally false and slanderous is his yarn that De Leon "tried to infiltrate the labor movement—just like the followers of Mr. [Wm. Z.] Foster today," and that he (De Leon) "used every sort of dirty slander ...." This wretched renegade and slanderer knows that he cannot produce one scrap of evidence to back up this false and cowardly charge. On the contrary, it was the associates of Bohn who resorted to the most fantastic lies when they found themselves unable to meet De Leon's logic, unable to refute the damning factual indictment he brought against the corrupt labor leaders and the equally corrupt "Socialist party" politicians, as well as the "veiled dynamiters," as De Leon designated Bohn's fellow anarcho-syndicalists in the post-1908 I.W.W. In thus slandering and lying about De Leon, "Dr." Bohn shows himself to be as unscrupulous and unprincipled in his dotage as he was in his "nonage."

It will be recalled that Bohn included Debs among

the "fighting American moralists" in the "great" tradition of the bully, "Teddy" Roosevelt, and the capitalist labor lieutenant *par excellence,* Sammy Gompers. This is a gross insult to Debs, who (whatever his faults and shortcomings) was basically an honest and sincere man who detested all that Teddy Roosevelt and Sam Gompers represented. It would be unfair not to recognize that Debs, though guilty of lapses and inconsistencies, fought the corruption in the S.P., and the politicians who, while gushingly expressing their love for him, inwardly cursed him and his "vagaries" on trade unionism, etc. At any rate, Debs, now hailed by Bohn as one of his heroes, again and again gave the lie to Bohn's brazenly false assertions about De Leon.

10

Debs's Tributes
To De Leon
And the S.L.P.

By way of completing this exposure of a menda-
cious renegade, it may not be amiss to cite a few in-
stances of Debs' respect for the S.L.P. and Daniel De
Leon. At the first convention of the I.W.W. (1905)
Debs (turning to De Leon and addressing him as
"Comrade") said:

"We have not been the best of friends in the past,
but the whirligig of time brings about some wonderful
changes. I find myself breaking away from some men
I have been in very close touch with, and getting in
close touch with some men from whom I have been
very widely separated."

With obvious reference to De Leon, Debs wrote
the following in the *Appeal to Reason* (April 12,
1912):

"It is foolish to say that the Socialist Labor Party
is dead. It is not dead, and for my part I do not want
to see it die. . . . Many of my early lessons in economics were taught me by that little 'bunch of fanatics,' and
I am not the least ashamed to admit it. . . . I can never
forget that little band of valiant comrades—frenzied
fanatics if you please, but still of the stuff out of which
revolutions are made. For years they were a mere
handful, and yet they fought as if they had legions be-

hind them. Staunchly they upheld the red banner in the face of an indifferent or hostile world—and this, years before some of those who now scoff at them had shed their bourgeois politics. There are not many of them, but few as they are, they have the backbone to stand alone. There are no trimmers or traders among them."

Again in the *National Ripsaw* (Vol. 8, No. 5), of which he was editor, Debs wrote the following:

"Upon that subject [of Socialist Industrial Unionism] we believe the Socialist Labor Party to be right. It does not palter with craft unionism, nor compromise for the purpose of currying favor with craft-union officials, but it takes its stand squarely for the revolutionary industrial organization of the workers, the only stand consistent with a revolutionary political party. Industrial organization is the foundation of the revolutionary movement, and without such organization political action is in vain and industrial democracy remains a dream."

In these and similar utterances Eugene Debs, in effect, rams the slanders and lies of Bohn down his brazen throat. However, the important point here is that if De Leon was a Communist (in the current Stalinist meaning of the term) then so was Debs. (And, to repeat, so was Bohn himself!) Yet Debs is a saint in Bohn's book, whereas De Leon is (or was) the Evil One incarnate!

The ordinary renegade and stoolpigeon is a repulsive creature, but doubly repulsive is he who (to protect the rewards of his treachery) turns traitor on his own past, and at the same time attempts to smear an illustrious personage with the very folly or crimes of which he himself has been guilty, and which the victim of his slanders opposed relentlessly. There is no suitable language in which to describe such infamy and unmitigated immorality. This double treason may bring the end. It is unlikely that a Bohn will be long remembered after he passes on, except possibly in infamy, rewards of a kind, but it is obviously self-defeating in whereas the name of Daniel De Leon will be remembered as long as an emancipated working class recognizes the virtue of gratefulness. For by laboring unselfishly, fruitfully and honorably in behalf of the exploited and oppressed working class, Daniel De Leon earned their undying gratitude, even as the tribe of the Bohns has earned the contempt that all well-informed, decent people bestow on "renegadoes, who . . . . are bound in conscience to be double knaves."

Selected
DE LEON EDITORIALS
on
The Struggle
Against
Bourgeois Socialism

From Harper's Weekly—Drawn by E. W. Kemble.

W. J. B.—SAY DEBS, HE'S HOOKED EVÉRYTHING THAT BELONGED TO ME, AND NOW HE'S GONE OFF WITH YOURS.

W.J.B. [Wm. Jennings Bryan] "Say, Debs, he [Teddy Roosevelt] has hooked everything that belonged to me, and now he's gone off with yours."

(The New York "Evening Sun," Sept. 20, 1912)

Appendix

THE CLASS STRUGGLE WITHIN THE PARTY

(The People, July 16, 1899)

[Speech by Daniel De Leon delivered on July 2, 1899, at a meeting of Party members to discuss issues before the Party.]

The editor of the *Volkszeitung* and his agents have counted without their host. In this debate they have taken up their full time with vilifications and slanders of the Party and myself. Their plan was to lure me away from the real issue, and have me take up my time refuting personalities. I shall not spend a minute on that.

Ehrenpreis said well: "The issue is the hostile principles of two hostile elements within the Party." These two elements have developed strongest in New York, the movement being here oldest. There is no such thing as "patching up" between them; one or the other must surrender unconditionally. What is the dividing line? To designate that, to characterize the two, and point out all that the division implies, I can do no better than quote the members of the editorial management of the *Volkszeitung* themselves. Grunzig, Jonas, Schlueter, each of them has at several times said to me, in answer to my enthusiasm for the Party: "Oh, it will never be the S.L.P., some other party will rise and do the work!" Do you realize what that means? In a Party such as this, the development of two elements, the one having abiding faith, the other having no faith in the future and effectiveness of the organization, is bound sooner or later to array the two in hostile camps against each other. At first, the difference is not felt; but in the measure that the element that HAS faith in the Party pushes on and becomes aggressive, the element that HAS NO SUCH FAITH is incommoded; and the time comes when the latter element, finding unbearable the demands put upon it by the aggressive element, beats around for pretexts to justify its inactivity and finally rises in rebellion. That time has come.

That this is no mere theory I shall prove to you out of Schlueter's own mouth, and with unquestionable facts of recent occurrence. In trying to explain away, at the last meeting, the charge of having suppressed matters favorable to the Party, Schlueter made three defenses:

FIRST DEFENSE—"I am not bound to take all such matter into the *Volkszeitung.*"—A Party editor, who HAS faith in the Party's future, a loyal editor, DOES feel so bound; he is greedy after matter favorable to the Party. One, on the contrary, who HAS NO SUCH FAITH, a disloyal Party editor, he, of course, DOES NOT feel himself under, has no sense of, any such obligation.

SECOND DEFENSE—"The matter was frequently treated by the *Vorwaerts* in such a style that I could not use the article."—Quite possible; every one has his own style of presenting a thing; one man's style is often distasteful to another; that sentiment must be respected. But a Party editor with faith in the Party's future, a loyal editor, feels in such a case BOUND to use such facts, presented in a style that he disapproves of, and take the trouble himself to write an article upon them in the style that suits him. An editor, on the contrary, who has no such faith, a DISLOYAL Party editor, HE feels himself under no such obligation; TO HIM that would be "too much bother"; HE takes it easy.

THIRD DEFENSE—"I could not vouch for the facts mentioned in *The People*."—Again, this is a consideration that deserves respect; the editor of a paper must feel sure of the facts he publishes; false facts would rather injure. But a Party editor, with faith in the Party's future, a LOYAL, conscientious editor, feels BOUND to verify such facts. An editor, on the contrary, with no such faith, a DISLOYAL Party editor, runs away from work; HE does not fill the office for the Party's sake; HE ducks his head, lets the facts slide—and draws his salary.

But all this is only the "little end" of the horn, symptomatic enough of such element, but yet only the "little end" of the horn in the development. From not "feeling bound" to take in everything, from "not feeling bound" to exert themselves in behalf of the Party, the element that has no faith in the Party develops disloyaltyward. The next step is a readiness to give the enemy "the benefit of the doubt." You all know the defense of the Carey-Debs Democracy in the matter of their Armory record, to wit, that if Carey had not voted for the $15,000 armory appropriation a heavy fine would have followed. How did Schlueter treat the matter? He gave the defense in full and then, editorially, added that he was not qualified to judge upon its correctness—and his supporters support him in this! Think of it, a Party editor, within six hours' ride of

Haverhill, "unqualified" to pass judgment upon so stupidly infamous and infamously stupid a defense! The element that HAS faith in the Party feels its pulse beat with indignation at such a "defense," and no effort is too much for it to make in order to confute the rascal Armoryites. The element, on the contrary, that HAS NO FAITH in the Party, the element and editor that are on the lookout for a "new party" to rise, they, of course, find it in keeping with their sentiments to "be gentle" with such miscreants, possibly the expected "new party"—and thus the irritation is increased while the lines are being drawn sharper between them.

The element that has no faith in the Party presently begins to tamper with the Party's principles and policy, while still pretending fealty to it. This is happening on the subject of the Party's trade union policy. From Schlueter down, you have seen them take up and hug to their hearts the closing words of the declaration, adopted at the last National Convention, which endorses the Alliance and urges the Party membership to carry the revolutionary spirit into the unions; and, turning their eyes heavenward, they meekly asked: In what way have we violated the Party declaration? A partial truth is the worst lie. They know they are garbling the Party's utterances. The passage they quote is only the conclusion of an argument, the premises of which declare the A. F. of L. and K. of L. to be hopelessly corrupt and the buffers for capital against the endeavors of the working class. The Party stands squarely upon these principles; the element that has faith in it upholds them with enthusiasm, despite troubles and inconveniences; the element, on the contrary, that has no faith in the Party, tries to ignore them and, despite their re-endorsement throughout the land, struggles against them as inconvenient, even to the extent of misquoting the Party, and demands that we "bore from within."

And yet this is not all. The element that has no faith in the Party, that, accordingly, is extremely punctilious about first "being able to vouch" for the facts furnished by other Party papers, that element is seen taking the "facts," furnished by bourgeois Democratic party papers, without verification, and liking them so well as even to multiply them by three, thus trying to make the workers believe that they pay $100 taxes a year, in violation of all fact and all science, and thus playing directly into the enemy's hands. And finally we find that element reaching, logically enough, the point of trampling the Party platform under foot, as they do in this matter of taxation, and going even so far as attempting to make the Party in this country subordinate to the party in Germany. That is their contention when the Party platform, which upholds the unquestionable principle that the taxes come from that part of the products of labor that labor is fleeced of anyhow by the capitalist class, is rubbed under their noses. You have heard Stahl on that subject. He no longer pretends to have respect for the platform. He asked: Was that platform ever submitted to a general vote? And his confreres, the *Volkszeitung* Germans, answered *"Nein!"* (No), and, accordingly, care not to uphold that platform. I ask: Were any of the German platforms, from which are taken the local pro-taxation planks that they quote, ever submitted to a general vote of the party in Germany? No! There is no referendum in the German party. There the party conventions decide, their decision is final. Think of the degrading position to which they want to lower the Party of America! The platform, adopted here, is to be treated as null because, forsooth, it was not submitted to a referendum, but the platform declarations of Germany, never adopted here and never submitted to a referendum even there, they are to be binding here! Altogether a position in keeping with total disrespect for, and no faith in, our Party! The other element, however, that HAS faith in our Party, respects the Party, holds high its platform and banner, and moves on convinced that the S.L.P. IS THE Party of emancipation in America. (Hisses from the *Volkszeitung* element.) Did you hear those hisses? They prove my case. THESE PEOPLE hiss the Party; we applaud it.

What is at the bottom of this marked difference? We cannot afford to be Socialists in one corner of our mouths, and fools in the other. We recognize the fact that material interests determine man's views. When we apply this scientific principle, every capitalist numskull politician charges us with being "personal." The charge of "personality" should never deter us. In this case, we need not look far for the material interests that determine the views and shape of the element within the Party that arrays itself against us, the element that HAS faith in the Party. Hergat in the Association, the board of directors before our National Executive Committee, were both outspoken. "The *Volkszeitung*," they declared, "cannot live without the support of the 'conservative' (read pure and simple) German unions." That is tip enough for anyone. Every pure and simpler with a job or expecting a job on a label committee or strike committee; every pure and simpler who fears for his sick and death benefit; all such are incommoded by the Alliance. Like veritable caricatures of the middle class, they clutch their "illusion of property," scared to death about losing it. They are willing to let the faker ride them and to stand by him, and they stand in dread of the Alliance, hence "feel quite sure that the S.L.P. cannot be the Party of the future." Again every one of them who has a little lager beer saloon, or a small store, or who, being a small trader, suffers, as the middle class generally, from the effects of taxation—all such think it execrable that the Party should not share the declarations of the Democratic party on taxation to the effect that the working class is crushed by taxes, and hence their views that not the S.L.P. but some other party must come to do the work—hence also their hisses for the Party.

It may be asked: Have the orators of that element also middle class, small property or pure and simple interests to guard? No. But on the same principle that the bourgeoisie attracts to itself as its orators a stripe of men of certain kindred intellectual interests, so likewise does the element that, for the reasons just given, "has no faith in the S.L.P.," attract to itself men whose interests run in somewhat similar grooves. For instance, it is no accident that among these spokesmen is a Schlueter—only a temporary sojourner in this land, awaiting the expiration of the sentence against him to return to his home in Germany; it is no accident that among these spokesmen is a Dr. Halpern (who acted at the last meeting as the claque for the traducers of the Party and its officers)—a gentleman whose jovial countenance we may at any time miss from our midst, his heart being in Russia, whither he pants to return as soon as it may be safe to do so; it is no accident that among these spokesmen is a Feigenbaum—a member who only the other day was seeking to perfect arrangements whereby he could fall on his feet back in Europe; it is no accident that among these spokesmen is a Nathan T. Stone—a young man who is pulling the wires for a job in McKinley's Agricultural Department, etc., etc. These are no accidents. A movement such as ours can be truly at the heart of those to whom, whether born here or not, America is their home; it can be truly at the heart of those only who look for no favors from the foe. To all others the movement can only be a sport or pastime. To such the aggressive, uncompromising spirit of the Party is either a "nuisance" or a hindrance in their schemes. None such can have any faith in the S.L.P., all such are bound eventually to run up against those who DO have faith in the S.L.P. and an "unpatchable-up" conflict is inevitable. When such a conflict does finally break out, it breaks out with force, and must be fought out to a definite settlement. The element that HAS faith in the Party is not of a temper to allow itself to be hamstrung, nor is it in the movement for the fun of the thing.

In this connection, the "violence of *The People's* attack" has been complained about. How silly! *The People* is not a monthly magazine for abstract philosophy, it is a weapon for concrete warfare. Whatever interferes with the sweep of the sword only adds to its vehemence. Let me initiate you into a bit of my experience:

It was in '94. The People's party of this city was trying to harmonize the "reform forces," and Section New York was invited to a conference. At the conference were, besides the Pops, free-traders, single-taxers, prohibitionists, and D.A. 49 of the then K. of L. I don't know how it came about but Section New York elected a delegation, Jonas and myself among them. As soon as the conference met, the discussion broke out upon the platform to be adopted; harmony was evidently impossible among such incongruous elements. Then rose Jonas and, to my surprise, proposed that the Pops and we agree upon a common ticket for the approaching campaign. I felt a chill run down my back. Had Jonas's proposition prevailed, it would have been the death of the S.L.P.; the Party could not have survived the spectacle of its candidates standing on the Populist ballot, and Populist candidates on ours; with the inevitable downfall of Populism, the S.L.P. would have been dragged down too, it would have been the pitiable thing that it was after a similar experience with the Greenback party; the work would have had to be started all over anew. Jonas's proposition failed, and the conference finally broke up for good. But the injury done to the Party by Jonas's proposition, THAT did not pass off so quickly. We Socialists were at the time struggling in D.A. 49 for the supremacy that we finally won, and Jonas's proposition acted there like a stick thrown between our legs. It matters not how violently a non-Socialist adversary may oppose a Socialist, provided he knows that he is opposing Socialism; if, however, he imagines that what the Socialist speaks for is not Socialism, then our work of agitation becomes infinitely harder. Jonas's proposition did that. In D.A. 49 workingmen stood up—our new esteemed Comrade Kinneally, here present, among them—who pointed the finger at me declaring: "Socialism is not against fusion; Jonas is for fusion, and he is a Socialist of old standing; your opposition to fusion is not Socialism." And there were those who went about saying that I had prevented fusion out of personal interest, not out of Socialist principle, seeing that Jonas, about whom clung the superstition that he was a pillar of uncompromising Socialism, was quite willing to fuse. Unnecessary to say that the Party's work in the hands of its English [language] agitators was not thereby aided; an intensification of work became necessary.

The same thing occurred when the *Volkszeitung's* campaign of bourgeois economics on taxation was started. Confronted by its declarations, as those of a "Socialist paper of old standing," our agitators would have been swept off the stump, and the burden of resistance would necessarily have been focused upon *The People.* The sword did what was natural and its bounden duty to do: it struck with redoubled force— all the stronger as it had become evident that a conspiracy was coming to a head through which the element "that has no faith in the Party" meant to save itself, i.e., its pure and simple or its bourgeois interests, by a *coup de main* and bagging the Party. The vigilance of the Party's administration has made certain that the conspiracy will suffer shipwreck.

TEN YEARS LATER, 1889-1899
(The People, July 23, 1899)

Under the title "Ten Years Later," Dumas wrote one of his most interesting, instructive and thrilling historical novels. The historic tale to be unfolded here in this article under the identical title may be found equally interesting, instructive and thrilling, if not more so, and inspiring besides to the student, especially the lover of the movement in America.

Ten years ago, the Socialist Labor Party was a "party" in name only. It is essential to a political party, first, that it be a pulsation of the national life of the country itself in which the party springs up; and, secondly, that it be politically active. That which ten years ago called itself the "Socialist Labor Party" lacked both essentials. The organization was not born of the throbbings of life in America; it was the result of political turmoils in Germany; in the quarry of American political development, it was not a formation of this soil. The organization was like gravel that one often finds upon ground of different geologic formation, shot off thither by volcanic eruptions from distant parts. As an inevitable result thereof, political activity, or anything deserving the name, was excluded. The membership located mainly in New York, limited itself to "agitation"—after a style; but they knew not their ground, evoked no response, and, owing to the frequently repulsive mannerisms of their principal spokesmen, were often even laughed at and despised; they grew disheartened; the less intellectually honest, vainer and less informed, like Alexander Jonas, Julius Grunzig, Hermann Schlueter and others, imputed their failure, not, as in fact, to their own shortcomings, but, to use their own words, to the "hopeless stupidity and corruption of the American people"; and thus, by degrees, the "Party" shrank into social clubs—singing and drinking and card-playing societies, with an occasional outing when a member died, and periodical celebrations in which thrilling speeches were delivered by themselves to themselves.

While this development was going on, there were others setting in also. Years ago the earnings of labor were higher; a thrifty mechanic, who did not object to pinching himself some, could lay by money in the bank. With the development of the capitalist system, earnings declined, savings became harder to make and jobs rarer to get.

Driven out of the shop by improved machinery and concentrating capital, the workingmen with savings in the bank fell back upon that, and started small stores, in short, rebounded into the middle class. One of the results of that—the seeming increase of the middle class—stumped the unscientific mind. The German Socialist, Edward Bernstein, concluded Marx was wrong, and the vulgar economists everywhere started new songs on the beauties of capitalism. Another result— the one we are here concerned with—was the changing of the angle of vision of the former workingman, who had become bourgeois. Speaking only a few years ago of the intellectual decline of the German Social Democracy, August Bebel referred to the numerous workingmen in Germany, who, being victimized by reason of their political activity, had to be provided with small stores by the German party, and, with their change of class interests, slid off from their pristine clear-cut radicalism. The economic development of capitalism here, above referred to, that caused workingmen with deposits to become small traders, wrought a like change in them. The change told strongly among certain German workingmen.

There is a third development that needs mention.

It is akin to the one last considered. The worker who had some savings, when thrown on the street by machinery, could fall back upon his savings and become bourgeois; the worker who had none stood on the ragged edge of the abyss of labor fakerism. Into that abyss fell not a few. Their unions became reactionary "pure and simple"; all sense of solidarity vanished; there was no longer a question of organizing and protecting the working class; the union became a means for those in it to get a job by and to put others out of their jobs; and finally it ripened into an engine of capitalism, sold to the politicians by the leading fakers.

Now, then, all these interests—the German labor faker, the German bourgeois ex-workingman and the singing, etc., society tired-out Socialist—clustered in this city around and centered in a German paper that, sailing under the name of Socialism, was, from its inception, essentially a practical business enterprise for its own employees. That paper was the *New Yorker Volkszeitung.*

The fishiness of the *Volkszeitung* was too rank to be concealed. Accordingly, about fourteen years ago, the "Party" element that was sound in mind and heart found it advisable to establish a bona fide Party organ in the German language—*Der Sozialist,* subsequently named *Vorwaerts,* a weekly paper—and later managed to acquire another weekly, in the English language, named the *Workman's Advocate.* The editors of these two papers, Rosenberg and Bushe, respectively, were like the rest of the "Party's" national officers, weak, insignificant men, wholly unfit for their responsible posts. Nevertheless, with all their unfitness, Rosenberg and Bushe saw a glimmer of light. A political party that is not in politics struck even them as absurd. Accordingly, ten years ago, they began to pull for political action. This was immediately to run foul of the *Volkszeitung.* The political field acts as a purifier; it makes havoc of false pretenses. The *Volkszeitung* was the "organ of the S.L.P." in this city. More or less labored articles on Socialism did it no harm, and an occasional good word for the then misnomer of a Socialist Labor Party was profitable. Without these monkeyshines the paper could not, as it was doing, drain the Party of funds—funds drained under the pretense of "upholding the Party press." That was all right. But actual politics, the putting up of an S.L.P. ticket and thus "hostilizing customers and advertisers" (AMONG THE LATTER OF WHOM POLITICAL CANDIDATES OF THE CAPITALIST PARTIES APPEARED not infrequently)—that was a horse of a different color, that would not do!

The *Volkszeitung* forthwith began to nag at the then editors of the Party organs. Rosenberg and Bushe, being the lightweights they were, allowed themselves to be angered, and finally driven into a preposterous, wholly untenable and mischievous position. Having got them there, and thus isolated from the rest of the "Party" members, whom the deep villainy of the *Volkszeitung* intrigue escaped, the *Volkszeitung* crowd rose in self-righteous indignation. "Something had to be done quick"; "the Party had to be saved," and more such cant, until, the "Party" membership having been seasoned by such a campaign of perfidy, the *Volkszeitung* crowd found it safe to carry out their scheme. One night they broke into the Party's premises, took the two papers and all their belongings, sacked the two editors, and bounced the National Executive Committee—and that was the end of that, in 1889.

Ten years have rolled by since—ten years equivalent to fifty. The very necessity that the *Volkszeitung,* together with its disreputable appendages, was under to disguise its real purpose behind a false issue, left it uncovered against the real danger that it had sought to escape—POLITICAL ACTION BY THE S.L.P.

At the same time that the affairs of '89 were going on in the "Party," a Socialist movement, to the manner born, was being throbbed into existence by the throbs of the nation itself. That movement went into the existing S.L.P., and transformed it. The very next year it unfurled its banner in the political field and held it. The *Volkszeitung* element was defeated. They valiantly sought to accommodate themselves to the inevitable, but could not; bankruptcy began to stare the *Volkszeitung* in the face; every year that passed made their element's position more unbearable. In front, the accelerated development of capital rendered the labor faker and the taxpaying small trader more and more desperate, while the magnificent progress of the Party, with its increasing revolutionary ardor, was burning them in the rear. For some time the foul interests of ten years ago had been plotting to ease their straits; their maneuvers to nag the Party's officers into blunders suffered shipwreck one after the other, and were turned upon them; then, all else proving unavailing, they staked their all upon a headlong coup that should strangle the Party—and failed ignominiously. Self-pilloried before the membership of the whole country as shameless violators of the Party constitution; beaten back, in the battle of the 10th instant, from the Party's

premises that they now again sought to capture by surprise and violence—all as narrated in last week's issue;
and subsequently outgeneraled in their attempts to
starve the Party and bar it from the post office, they
are today, July, '99, a physically and morally shattered
crew.

*

The year '99 is ten years later than '89. The S.L.P.
is no longer a social club located mainly in New York.
Within the last ten years its inspired apostles and its
press have, with words of fire, cast abroad the rejuve-
nating spark, kindled the flame of classconsciousness in
America, and planted the standard of the Social Revolution in the land. The S.L.P. has become a Party, indeed; it has leaped the boundaries of the city and
state; it has spread out north, south and west, and now
extends from ocean to ocean, honored, respected,
feared, over 80,000 strong.

In 1899, the S.L.P. is no longer the concern that
can be bagged by the canaille of capitalist society.

MILKSOPS OR MEN

(Daily People, June 5, 1910)

When told that the planks of his Social Democratic
party are all reform planks, and that the old parties
will steal them from him, Victor L. Berger is reported
to have answered: "Let them steal them; we shall
manufacture new planks faster than they can steal
them."

There is some truth in this answer, also solid error;

besides that, considerable misprision of plutocratic interests.

The truth in Mr. Berger's answer lies in the fact that reform is infinite, in distinction to revolution, which is finite. There is no end to measures for the padding of the yoke of slavery. Clean streets, hygienic tenements, seats in cars, free music in parks—the list of these is endless. No doubt such paddings to the yoke of wage slavery could be prolonged indefinitely, at least theoretically. But does it follow that the paddings will bring Socialism one inch nearer? By no means.

The same "humanity" that taught our savage ancestors that it was less profitable to slaughter their conquered foes, eat a goodly number of them, and leave the rest to rot, than it was to let up on work themselves, and turn their captives into slaves to do the toiling; the identical "humanity" that taught our nearer predecessors that kind treatment to animals paid, and that blossomed into institutions for the prevention of cruelty to animals; the identical "light" that only yesterday fell upon the mind's eye of the Kaiser when he turned over a new leaf in the matter of open-air meetings, called off his police, and allowed the masses to give vent to the pent-up steam of their resentment; that identical "humanity" will teach and that identical "light" will enlighten the minds of the employing class to the effect that a well fed, well housed and musically entertained wage slave yields more wool than an underfed, badly housed and unentertained one.

The lesson once taught, the light once seen, the tables will immediately be turned upon the "Socialist" manufacturer of reform planks. Instead of the "Socialist" reformers' being the manufacturers, and the employers' parties the "ultimate consumers" of these planks, the employers' parties will become the manufacturers, outstrip the "Socialist" reformers, and turn the latter into the "ultimate consumers" of the output. It is in the cards that the day is bound to come when what Mr. Berger now says of his party, the employers will confidently say of their own: "We shall manufacture new planks faster than the S.D.P. can steal them." When that day comes, the Bergers will find themselves in the plight of the deserted Gaius Gracchus. A following trained at the milk bottle of reform is bound to develop into weaklings and milksops.

There is but one plank for the Socialist to manufacture, one that the capitalist could no more steal than a mouse can steal a cat—the abolition of wage slavery. There is but one plank that trains men and not milksops—unconditional surrender of the capitalist class.

GETTING SOMETHING NOW
(Daily People, September 6, 1910)

The *New Yorker Volkszeitung,* an organ of the Socialist party, in its issue of September 3, editorially ventures "to propose" to its "party's executive committee to utilize [Theodore] Roosevelt's thunder—which anyhow is stolen from us—for the Socialist [Socialist party] fall campaign." The same editorial says of the electors, "They are also little benefited, at present, by the Socialist goal."

Roosevelt may or may not have stolen Socialist party "thunder"; he, however, stole nothing from Socialism. That he stole or cared to steal Socialist party "thunder" is pretty good evidence of the fate that is in store for the Socialist party. And that the hand of fate is upon the S.P. is confirmed by the *Volkszeitung's* own declaration as to the "little benefit" that can be secured at present from the Socialist goal.

The theory that the success of Socialism is predicated upon the movement's gaining something for the workers *now,* right away, is a theory that has no place in the program of revolutionary Socialism, especially in America.

The fundamental principle of Socialism is that freedom for the workers is not possible while the system of wage slavery lasts. Hence Socialism has for its mission the overthrow of the capitalist system of private ownership of the machinery of production and the establishment of collective ownership in its place.

The theory that Socialism can with safety depart from the hard and fast line of its ultimate goal and follow the lure of "something now" batters itself against the hard fact that "something now" is not obtainable by it, and the logical consequence of such departure would be the degeneration of the movement into a "something now," or reform, movement.

American history bears eloquent testimony to the fact that "something now" is not obtainable now. The fate of the movements that followed that lure into the desert of opportunism is to be read upon their gravestones as a warning to others.

If the aim of Socialism were to be made the getting of "something now" and Socialism later, Socialism would have to be sacrificed to immediate progress. Hence for a Socialist to preach "something now" means that he discredits Socialism, and only helps to prepare the workers as voting cattle for capitalism, when capitalist parties, by "stealing," by taking up the "something now" demands, promise their immediate realization.

The Socialist party that in America follows the lure of getting "something now" will wind up by getting nothing now. Nor will it get anything later, because it will have lost the golden opportunity of preparing the workers and the way for the benefits of the Socialist goal.

The only something worth striving for now by Socialists, because it is the only thing obtainable now, is the laying of as solid a foundation as possible on which to move forward to the conquest of capitalism. Then, too, the more attention that Socialists pay to the ultimate goal, the more will the capitalist class endeavor to stem the tide and check its progress by offering "something now" schemes galore; so that, granting that "something now" is desirable, the way to get it is not by bothering about it but by working steadily for the goal.

The *Volkszeitung* and other S.P. papers have thrown Socialism to the winds and become a rainbow-chasing institution. If such doctrine is accepted and practiced by the Socialist party, it will ere long be interred with the other rainbow-chasers, upon whose headstones is to be read the inscription, "I tried to get 'something now' and got here."

STEALINGS OF THUNDER
(Daily People, August 13, 1912)

The press of the Socialist party is throwing fits, partly of rage, partly of girlish giddy-headed vainglory, because Roosevelt has stolen their thunder.

Who is it that "steals thunder"?

A tailor cannot steal the thunder of an astronomer; a carpenter cannot steal the thunder of a lawyer; a prima donna cannot steal the thunder of an excavator. The reason is obvious. While each of these has a "thunder" of his own, the "thunder" of one is not available to the other; it does not fit the other's "line."

The supplemental phenomenon is noticed on the political field. Republicans steal "thunders" from Democrats; Democrats steal "thunders" from Republicans; both steal "thunders" from Prohibitionists; and Prohibitionists, as the "broad-gauge" and "narrow-gauge" varieties, respectively, did in the first Bryan campaign, steal "thunders" from their Democratic and Republican foes. And so forth.

The uniformity of the incapacity to steal "thunder," in the one set of instances, and of the practice of "thunder stealing," in the other set of instances, establishes the law that underlies "thunder stealing." The stealing of thunder can be done only by kindred spirits from kindred spirits. Where no such kinship exists, no "thunder" can be stolen; where "thunder" is stolen, stealer and stealee are kith and kin.

Roosevelt certainly has stolen the "thunder" of the Socialist party. The statement to that effect made by Democrats and standpat Republicans is no libel upon the Socialist party—except in the sense that "the greater the truth, the greater the libel." Moreover, in this instance there can be no question of libel. The "Socialists," whose thunder Roosevelt is said to have stolen, are admitting the charge.

"State Socialism"—a term, we think, of Bismarckian coinage—is purely technical. It designates the social regimen in which the capitalist class, having advanced far enough to "feel its oats," drops the mask that its political government is "by, of and for the people"; comes out with the truth that its political rule is by, of and for the top capitalist; and is ready, "plump and plain," to disclose the fact by publicly, organically identifying its political agents with its corporation directors. There may be guile, and probably is, in the choice of the term "State Socialism" to designate sublimated capitalism. But, guile or no guile, there is as much Socialism in "State Socialism" as there would be drunkenness in "State prohibitionism," or protection in "State free trade." Everyone who knows anything knows that.

The long list of facts with which the Socialist Labor Party has demonstrated that there is nothing of Socialism but the name in the Socialist party, and that the party is essentially bourgeois; the long list of facts with which the Socialist Labor Party has demonstrated that the officialdom and press of the Socialist party only speculate on the word Socialism; the long list of facts with which the Socialist Labor Party has demonstrated that the path on which the said officialdom and press lead the working class is the path to the shambles; the long list of facts with which the Socialist Labor Party has demonstrated that the said officialdom and press conduct themselves with Socialism in the way of wild Indians who have found a watch, and who, having had "their day" of silly triumph, would find themselves "left"—those long lists are now confirmed by the event.

Those long lists are now confirmed by the historic

event of the phenomenal apparition of the Roosevelt party on the nation's stage; they are now confirmed by the fits of rage that the officialdom and press of the Socialist party are throwing at the prospect of forfeiting and losing "thousands and even hundreds of thousands of votes," because of their "thunder's" being stolen; they are being confirmed by the fits of girlish giddy-headed vainglory that the said officialdom and press are throwing at the discovery that their "thunder" is considered valuable enough to be stolen. The revolutionary party whose thunder can be stolen by the class against which it takes the field had better quit.

"SOCIALISM" IN MILWAUKEE

(Daily People, January 25, 1911)

The Hon. Victor L. Berger, Social Democratic Congressman-elect, informed an Oklahoma audience, as set forth in *Political Action* for January 21, that "not only are the masses with us [the Social Democratic administration of Milwaukee], but the businessmen are applauding."

Such a statement is calculated to cause the knowing to prick up their ears.

By "masses" must be understood the workers; by "businessmen" must be understood the skinners of the workers. That the two frequently go together is a deplorable social fact, due to class-unconsciousness on the part of the "masses" and to the deceptive language of the "businessmen." One of the tasks of Socialism is to undo the fact: to expose the deceptiveness of the "businessmen" and thereby open the eyes of the "masses."

Something must be out of the usual run if an administration boasting of its Socialism enjoys both the applause of the skinners and the support of the skinnees.

Either the "businessmen" have been seized upon by a Pentecostal fire; have dropped their class practices; have, in short, ceased to be skinners—truly a miracle.

Or the "Socialism" that is accompanied by the applause of "businessmen," without receiving the hootings and catcalls of the "masses," is the same old regulation bourgeois claptrap of reform decked in the trappings of Socialism—no miracle at all.

Which of the two explains the Milwaukee status as described by Congressman Berger?

It so happens that, together with the issue of *Political Action* quoted from, there reached this office a communication, printed elsewhere in this issue, from a Milwaukee correspondent, that helps solve the riddle.

Our correspondent sets forth that—squaring at all points with the bourgeois conception which looks down upon and degrades labor—the "Socialist administration" of Milwaukee is advancing the salaries of clerks who already received a bounteous wage, while it leaves the city's manual employees—men whom the city administration requires to work eight hours a day, six days a week, in rain or shine—with their noses to the starvation grindstone of $11 a week.

The riddle presented by Congressman Berger's account of the Milwaukee status is solved.

DEBS ON THE PROGRAM OF SOCIALISM
(Daily People, September 9, 1912)

Agreeable to the promise made last week, we now return to the statement made by Eugene V. Debs in the

Pittsburgh, Pa., *Press,* and submit it to closer scrutiny.

Mr. Debs cites "old-age pensions," "minimum wage," "industrial insurance" and "welfare of labor" as "part of the program of Socialism."

This is news.

Old-age pensions are no part of the program of Socialism. Long before Socialism was thought of, there were poorhouses.

The minimum wage is no part of the program of Socialism. Many a passage in Thorold Rogers' work, and in Green's history of the English people, not to mention less popular works, points clearly to the conclusion that from the time of the downfall of wages, the event that Thorold Rogers calls the "conspiracy against the workmen" after Edward the Second, movements of resistance sprang up with demands that are tantamount to a minimum wage. Surely there was not then the slightest thought of, let alone organization for, Socialism.

Industrial insurance is no part of the program of Socialism. The monasteries of the Middle Ages, with their hospital attachments and asylums for the poor, had the lead of Socialism in point of time by quite a roll of centuries.

Welfare of labor, in so far as it constitutes a plank of political parties in the land, will be found a hundred years ago by whosoever cares to trace the "sops to labor" back that far. There was no Socialism then.

The capitalist class is not always reckless of the two-legged cattle which, together with the four-legged ones, are needed for production. As there are bourgeois laws against "cruelty to animals," there were laws, early factory laws, initiated by capitalists to guard their labor working cattle. These laws were not the product of Socialism.

No doubt the programs of many, if not all, of the European parties of Socialism embrace demands for "old-age pensions," together with such other means to alleviate the sorrows of the wage slave class. That is due to the fact that in hardly one European country has the bourgeois as yet settled accounts with feudalism, and, consequently, Socialism in those countries is bound to reach outside its own program.

What the program of Socialism should be is best ascertained in countries like our own. Here the program of Socialism is the overthrow of the political State and the establishment of the Industrial Republic. Such a program denies conditions for labor pauperism. How alien from the program of Socialism, a program that demands the social revolution, palliations and "immediate demands" are is proven by Mr. Debs's own admission that Roosevelt has "burglarized" the platform of his party.

The program of revolution is revolution. Palliatives are props to that which the revolution intends to overthrow. No such prop can be within the contemplation, or form part of the program, of Socialism.

THREE S.P. FIGURES

(Daily People, December 20, 1910)

When the Socialist Labor Party—despite its much smaller vote and membership—maintains that its tactics, hence its principles, make it a permanency, whereas the Socialist party—its much larger vote and membership notwithstanding—is a transitory affair because of its heterogeneous tactics and principles, the S.L.P. states a double fact that is founded upon granite.

There are in the S.P. three leading figures—Berger, Haywood and Debs. What are the views they enunciate upon the vital issue of the economic organization, hence upon fundamental tactics and principles?

Victor Berger, most conspicuous as a "doer of things," has as his motto in his *Social Democratic Herald*:

WAGE EARNERS, WAKE UP!

Join the union of your craft and the party of your class— always demand the **union label** and shop card. Cast your ballots for emancipation from wage slavery.

William D. Haywood, distinguished as the incarnation of the proletariat,[1] expressed himself on Sunday, December 18, in the Yorkville Casino in this city as follows:

I want to say to you that no Socialist can be a trade unionist. The ethics of trade unionism forbid such a possibility. So-

---

[1] William D. Haywood was one of a trio of leaders of the Western Federation of Miners who had been arrested in Colorado in 1907 and illegally spirited to Idaho to stand trial for the murder of ex-Governor Steunenberg. Their case was a cause celebre in its day and aroused indignation throughout the labor movement. De Leon quickly recognized that the case had made Haywood a potential force for good in the movement. In a remarkable letter to Haywood on the occasion of the latter's acquittal (See "Daniel De Leon, A Symposium"), De Leon said: "The capitalist class has again wrought better for the social revolution than that class is aware—it has, through your now celebrated case, built you up for the work of unifying the movement upon sound ground." Alas, De Leon's hope that Haywood might rise to the opportunity was dashed. Haywood was a small man, incapable of playing the role for which circumstances had cast him. De Leon's reference to him as "the incarnation of the proletariat" unquestionably referred to the class struggle drama of 1907.

cialism proclaims the class struggle. When trade unionists enter into an agreement with the employer they are perpetuating the capitalist class and system for the time that the contract lasts.

Every trade unionist will swear that he hates the soldier and militiaman like poison. But who enlists to feed the soldier, to make bullets and guns for the militiaman? The trade unionist—when he signs a contract with the capitalist class!

Not only that, but the trade unionist makes the soldier himself. How? By the apprenticeship system. The number of apprentices is restricted. Fathers in the trade unions say to their sons: "You can't learn this trade." Thus the youth are forced out of an occupation into jail, the army and the navy. Why is this apprenticeship system? Because the trade unions are not unions but job trusts. They are ruled by craft, not class, consciousness.

They insist, again, on the closed shop. Closed to whom? Not to the boss. He has the key to the front door! The trade unionist closes the shop on the working class. I say open the union to all the workers, then you'll have the only closed shop worth having.

When the apprenticeship system does not suffice to keep out workers, the trade unions raise up an initiation fee—$50 to join the hod-carriers' union, $150 to join the electricians in Chicago, and even $500 to become a member of the glass bottle blowers. Do you yet see the necessity of organizing one labor union big enough to take in all the workers? The trade unions are not organized to fight the battles of the working class, they are organized to protect the few favored individuals fortunate enough to get inside the wall.

What we Industrialists propose is the organization of one union, not for America only, but big enough to wipe out all state and even national lines. We would organize according to industries. We are going to start the cooperative commonwealth, and we're not going to ask Milwaukee how to do it. The best they can do in Milwaukee is administer affairs in one small section of the public service department. That is not the whole industrial democracy by any means. For that the millions employed in food production, mining, manufacturing, transportation and every other industry must also be organized, instead of about one million as organized today.

And, as if all this were not yet clear enough, upon

the question's being asked him whether the Socialists in the A. F. of L. should leave that body and join the Industrial Union, Haywood considered the points and drove them home with the answer:

> I would so advise wherever the A. F. of L. was not able to deprive the worker of his bread and butter. Where the A. F. of L. controls your living, stay in it; where you are free to follow principle, join the Industrial Workers.

Finally, Eugene V. Debs, the party's orator, in a letter to Tom Mann published in the *International Socialist Review* for August, says:

> In answer to your direct inquiry I have to say that I, too, am opposed, like yourself, to undertaking to destroy the old unions. Such a policy can be fruitful only of mischief to Industrial Unionism, as we have reason to know on this side... Nor do I believe in organizing dual unions in any case where the old union substantially holds the field.

The "union of your craft" in Berger's motto, the "trade union" in Haywood's words, the "old unions" in Debs's letter—all refer to the same thing—the A. F. of L. and kindred unionism, pets of the Civic Federation. In their views on how to handle that "proposition," Berger stands at one extreme end, a rounder for the A. F. of L.; Haywood at the opposite end; Debs in the middle with a theory for avoiding mischief that all experience denies.

A revolutionary movement cannot be "all things to all men." Coalitions may serve movements aiming to reform a social system that is in existence, and the perpetuation of which is the object of reform. To a revolutionary movement coalitions are either checks to the march, or, if they do not check it from the start, they in the end obstruct it and throw it back demoralized.

The Debs posture of seeking peace where there is no peace is bungling. The Berger posture is at war with the law of evolution; A. F. of L. unionism is a blind alley. Only Haywood's posture is the true one because it alone fits all the facts; and that posture is, in the spirit and the letter, the posture of the S.L.P.

A. F. of L. unionism has become a fraud on the word union. Etymologically it is false—it disunites the working class; sociologically it is an obscene monstrosity: clad in the trappings of labor, it is the bulwark of capital. Capital, the unwilling handmaid of progress, is itself compulsorily sapping the foundations of A. F. of Hellishness. In the measure that capital does that, it strains to hedge in the now ever more hollow hull with superstitious reverence, with the reverence due to bona fide unionism only, a quality that, if the A. F. of L. ever possessed it, has long since fled from it.

It is the task, the imperative mission, of the Socialist, to supplement the work of capital by tearing down and demolishing the superstition. This message was first delivered, the *mot d'ordre* [word of command] was first sounded in the land by the Socialist Labor Party. To the task of carrying out that mission essential to Socialist progress and triumph, the S.L.P. has serenely bent to the oars, undeterred by the vindictiveness of its opponents, untouched by the poisonous arrows that flew and still fly thick upon it—untouched, because armored with integrity of purpose; undeterred because unerringly guided by the light of science to the only goal worth striving for by our generation, the emancipation of the working class, and thereby the final abolition of class rule.

Not the heterogeneity of a Japanese quilt, but, in

fundamentals, the homogeneity that insures unity of action can alone insure permanence to a party of Socialism. And that homogeneity must be planted upon the rockbed of fact, not upon the quicksand of illusion.

AN OPEN LETTER
(Weekly People, March 8, 1913)

To Franz Mehring,
Stuttgart, Germany.
Fellow Socialist—

We wish to thank you, in the name of the Socialist Labor Party, for the exposure you have made of John Spargo's unfitness as a biographer of Marx and an expositor of Marxism. The exposure was so complete that we reproduced it the week before last in these columns in English garb. We also wish to congratulate you upon being the first of the comrades in Germany to publicly demonstrate his freedom from the mental domination of that queer thing, known in this country as the American bourgeois bluff.

Plechanoff preceded you by about five years on the continent, among the Russian Socialists. Ernest Untermann—like Spargo a Socialist party member, and, like Spargo, a European immigrant of that sorry type that, incapable of acquiring the virtues of the American, readily adopts the vices of the American dealer in wooden nutmegs—threw the American bourgeois bluff of writing on the philosophy of the movement. His production being translated, Plechanoff took it up; tore it to shreds; and, as you are doing now with Spargo's book, threw the bits into the face of the bluffer, with the contempt that he deserves who, without intellectual fitness for so grave a subject, presumes to trifle with the movement by trying to bluff it into admiration for himself.

After that, until you broke the ice, a number of other men in the leadership of the party named "Socialist" in this country threw their American bourgeois bluff in the shape of "books" on the social question a la Spargo—and took in our unsuspecting comrades in Germany.

There was, first on the list in chronological order, Robert Hunter with a book in which the science of biology was insulted with the novel theory that, if the original 3,000,000 American colonists had only been left to themselves, the country would now be populated with their own descendants to the number of the ninety-odd million who now inhabit the land. In this book the flood of European immigration—an immigration that certainly saved our present population from being the mentally and physically feeble aggregation of people that they would otherwise be, had the original small number of colonists been left to any such intensive inbreeding—is insulted with the designation of degraded foreigners, and with the novel theory, to match, of laying at their door the practice of infanticide, for which the chauvinistic portion of the "old stock" American is noted. That bluff was translated in Germany by a Social Democrat with praises for "the great American sociologist."

Next came Morris Hillquit—better known in his original home as Moses Hilkowitz—with sundry "bluffs," also in the shape of books. One of these, calling itself the history of Socialism in America, was also translated by a German Social Democrat—a work that will convey to the German reader, who has only such a source of information on America, as topsy-turvy an idea of the Socialist movement in America, men and things, as Spargo's slap-dash work conveys of Marx; or as the books on the history of the republican Rome, that we are informed are gotten up in Russia by the agents of the Czar for consumption among the ignorant.

And now, to skip minor instances, comes Spargo's book upon Marx, which is also translated in Germany.

In its report to the Stuttgart Congress, the Socialist Labor Party stated that the battles of the American movement will have to be fought on American soil, and not in the columns of papers abroad. The principle is true; but all is not said when that is said.

International capitalism has brought about an international proletarian and Socialist movement, greatly promoted by modern facilities of communication and transportation. It goes without saying that, under such conditions, the movement in any one country cannot remain wholly unaffected by the movement in any other. The magnificence of the movement in Germany —where, because of the still surviving and powerfully surviving vestiges of feudalism, the Social Democracy is compelled to complete the unfinished progressive program of the German bourgeois revolution; and where, despite the tangle, the tactfulness of the Social Democracy has rendered it the "summa summarum" of all the progressive aspirations of Germany—cannot fail to affect the movement in America. That fact the Hunters, the Hillquits, the Spargos seek to utilize for ends of their own.

Your criticism of Spargo's book as "a worthless compilation," a "thing that workmen's libraries should be prevented from throwing their good money away on," an "insulting disregard of International Socialism" — that criticism fits all those other books, or wooden nutmegs, "bluffs," for short. Yet their authors rush to Europe, preferably to Germany; bluff the German comrades; get themselves translated; and then parade in this country with "the endorsement of the Social Democracy."

The psychology that renders our European comrades so liable to succumb is readily understood. In their anxiety to see a powerful movement in America, and having their own hands full with the vast issues that confront them there, they have little time to weigh things American. The dealer in Socialist wooden nutmegs catches them unawares. The "bluff" succeeds. The net result to the movement in America is that an even greater burden is thrown upon the shoulders of the militant Socialists of the land.

That you, a distinguished personality in the Social Democracy, have stood up, the first of our German fellow Socialists and condignly branded the American bourgeois and bluffer, earns our congratulations to you; at the same time our thanks.

May others, for the sake of Socialism, follow your example.

With Socialist greetings,

DANIEL DE LEON,

Editor, *Daily People*.

A POLITICAL FORECAST

(Daily People, February 4, 1913)

Concrete forecasts with regard to persons are pro-verbially risky. No forecaster can be posted upon all the factors bearing upon a certain individual that de-termine his ultimate conduct. Fully aware of the slip-pery ground on which he treads who seeks to peer into the future of an individual, nevertheless aware that, however far from the bull's-eye the forecast may fall, it will fall within the circle of the target provided the known facts are properly weighed, we venture the fore-cast that Colonel Theodore Roosevelt will some day be seen to call himself, and to chieftain a political move-ment styled, "Socialist."

We are not forgetful of the fact that Roosevelt has repeatedly been shown in these columns to be of the man-on-horseback temperament, and of the Caesar-ian mold in history. It is the cumulating evidences of this fact, joined with more recent developments, that suggest the eventual appearance of Roosevelt under a banner inscribed "Socialism." The combination — Roosevelt and Socialism — is, of course, baroque; but so is Roosevelt, and so are all the Roosevelts whom the waves of history have washed upon the shores of time.

Socialism, as he who knows anything knows, aims at human emancipation, not by political tenets, but by the establishment of material conditions upon which freedom can be planted. This implies a social revolu-tion. Nor is this all.

The social revolution implied in Socialism needs for

its success the action of the least favored of all present classes, and, what is more, of all revolutionary classes that have yet stepped upon the stage of history. The task of educating and organizing at least a necessary minimum of this revolutionary class with the minimum knowledge to resist the onslaught and, worst of all, the wiles, of the ruling class, is gigantic. Even the bourgeoisie in its pre-revolutionary era was frequently disintegrated by alternate applications of the feudal mailed and the feudal velvet-gloved fist. The bourgeoisie, however, could not be permanently broken up. Its strength lay in the growth of its economic power.

It is otherwise with the modern revolutionary classes. The proletariat declines in economic power. Accordingly, in the measure that proletarian might in numbers waxes, there increases proletarian precariousness of existence; hence, proletarian nervousness; hence, proletarian lack of self-reliance; hence, proletarian desperation; hence, proletarian proneness to superstition. Hand in hand with this progression goes, it is true, Socialist education counteracting the above-mentioned downward progression. Indeed, viewed from the angle of the sociologic tussle, modern society presents the spectacle of a race between Socialist education and proletarian demoralization. Which will succeed in heading off the other?

We hold that, properly weighed, the social influences of the day that make for proletarian education will triumph, and triumph gloriously. Notwithstanding this, the influences that make for proletarian demoralization are so vast that they must be reckoned with. These influences, together with their immediate product, a demoralized and submerged layer of the proletariat, not only heat into life but also attract certain sinister figures. Richard II, applying to Wat Tyler's mob for the privilege of being their leader; more recently, Louis Bonaparte starting, or utilizing, the "Society of December"; the "millionaire" Crassus of Roman days identifying himself with the rag-tag and bobtail that hugged Catiline and was hugged by him; the succession of "tyrants" in Greece and the Aegean Isles—these are many variants of an identical type. In all these instances, mass precariousness of existence begot mass nervousness; mass nervousness begot mass lack of self-reliance; mass lack of self-reliance begot desperation; and desperation begot superstition.

A superstitious mass in economic straits looks for saviors from "above." In Rome the savior was looked for from the senatorial rank; in other places, from the wealthy class. On the same principle that weak lungs are the point of gravitation for the tuberculosis microbe, such mass mentality is the point of gravitation for the tribe of the Roosevelts. Any flag will do for them; any device is good enough for their purpose. "Socialism" will not prove an unacceptable mantle within which, or flag under which, given the continuance of favorable conditions, Colonel Theodore Roosevelt may yet be seen braggadociating across the stage of the American social drama.

A SOWER WENT FORTH
(Daily People, December 28, 1909)

A correspondent illustrates with the names of several men and one woman a point he brings up that puzzles him. The point is:

"These persons are only a few of several whom I could name. Their minds started as utter blanks on the social question. They came in touch with the Socialist Labor Party, the *Daily* and WEEKLY PEOPLE, and the rest of the S.L.P.'s brilliant literature. Forthwith they became 'speakers' and even 'writers.'

"I watched them closely. They were parrots. I hoped that, from parroting, they would begin to digest the vast amount of sound principles they were taking in, but I saw no evidence of any such digestive process. On the contrary, I saw evidence of increased and increasing superficiality, accompanied by vanity and vainglory. And presently I saw them, one after another, fly off the handle, acting as though they knew it all, and making asses of themselves.

"What can be the cause of this? Can it be, I have often asked myself, that there is some defect in the method of S.L.P. literature so that, instead of its rendering these people solid thinkers, with a respect for knowledge and for the difficulty of acquiring the same, it causes many of them to become top-heavy, and to grow into impudent, insolent swaggerers? Of course, these are not the rule. But there are so many of them and they make so much noise that they have attracted my attention.

"I have asked myself the question: Can it be that this evil is the result of the distinctive virtue of S.L.P. literature, which is that S.L.P. literature presents the toughest knots of science in a style so easy that it can be unraveled by all? Did the figure cut by these people ever strike you?"

Our correspondent can best be answered with one

of the most poetic parables, and one withal true to nature, of the carpenter of Nazareth:

"A sower went forth to sow:

"And when he sowed, some seeds fell by the wayside, and the fowls came and devoured them up.

"Some fell upon stony places, *where they had not much earth; and forthwith they sprung up, because they had no deepness of earth*:

"And when the sun was up, they were scorched; and because they had no root, they withered away.

"And some fell among thorns; and the thorns sprung up, and choked them.

"But others fell into good ground, and brought forth fruit, some an hundredfold, some sixtyfold, some thirtyfold."

That sower is the S.L.P.; and the seeds it sows meet with all the accidents in the parable. Some of the seeds "fall by the wayside" and the foes of Socialism devour them; some of the seeds "fall among thorns" and the thorns of interested slummery and "intellectualism" choke them; and some of the seeds, *falling on shallow minds, forthwith spring up fast because they find no deepness of earth into which to cast their roots.* These are the elements our correspondent has in mind.

There is nothing the matter with the literature of the S.L.P. Our correspondent will admit that to prevent its shooting up where there is no deepness of earth would be to render it so sterile that it would be unable, when falling upon good ground, to bring forth the many hundredfold fruit that it is bound to bring forth in due season.

ANARCHO-BOURGEOIS RUFFIANISM
ON EXHIBITION

(Daily People, March 19, 1912)

As the wild goat is drawn to the hills, as the swine is drawn toward the swill, so "Direct Action" is drawn to ruffianism.

The fact was demonstrated in Boston on the fifteenth of this month, at the Paine Memorial Hall meeting addressed by William D. Haywood, as previously reported in these columns.

Haywood, in the course of his speech, administered merited chastisement to the Civic-Federationized and Militia-of-Christized John Golden. At the close of the meeting, Arthur Reimer, a wage-slave member of the National Executive Committee of the Socialist Labor Party, came forward to the platform, together with others, and addressed Haywood as follows: "Comrade Haywood, I heartily endorse your condemnation of the traitorous conduct of John Golden in going into the city of Lawrence during the strike and seeking to divide the workers on strike; but how do you justify your conduct in going to the city of Paterson last Thursday night, knowing as you did that there was a strike of the I.W.W.[1] silk workers on in Paterson, and from a public platform seeking to discredit the leader of that strike, Rudolph Katz?" Haywood's

---

[1] This reference is to the original I.W.W., known then also as the "Detroit I.W.W.," as distinguished from the Haywood anarcho-syndicalist I.W.W., which had stricken the political clause from its preamble.

first answer was: "Well, did you see the circular that Katz sent out?"

Obviously, Haywood did not know who Reimer was; obviously, Haywood thought Reimer might not be informed on the facts; obviously, Haywood sought to convey to Reimer the impression that the circular in question was a vicious one, so vicious as to provoke, cause and justify his coming to Paterson, whereas, as readers of the PEOPLE are aware, the circular was a firm but temperate presentation of the facts bearing on the occasion.

But Haywood's low cunning missed its mark. Reimer was thoroughly posted. So well posted that he immediately replied: "Yes; you mean the circular issued by Local 25, I.W.W., and there was nothing in that circular which would warrant your interference; and what is more, the circular was not issued until your coming was publicly announced."

The attempt to deceive having failed, "Direct Action" forthwith struck the second of its natural poses— ruffianism. As the report puts it: "Without a single word of warning, Haywood suddenly kicked his right foot, with all the force of his huge bulk behind it, into Reimer's chest." Then, not satisfied with that, he attempted again to hit the man whom his cowardly brutality had rendered helpless.

Guilty of having deliberately attempted to perpetrate against the I.W.W. striking silk weavers of Paterson the identical act that John Golden had attempted against the striking Lawrence mill hands, an act he [Haywood] had just been condemning—namely, stabbing them in the back; and finding his endeavor to play scuttlefish vain, the anarchist leaped forward in all his gorilla-like savagery, with the only argument that his nature knows.

Some may cry: "Bring the felonious assailant before the bar of the law!"

We say: "No! Bring him before a loftier tribunal —the bar of the Labor, or Socialist, movement. Hold him there, a specimen—and, no doubt, a specimen admired by his breed—of "Direct Action." Pillory, through him, that menace to Labor's integrity and progress—many-named and manifoldly disguised anarchy.

The pure and simple political Socialist lays all his stress upon the parliamentary epoch of "political action." The S.L.P. lays no stress whatever upon the parliamentary, but lays all its stress upon the pre-parliamentary or agitational epoch of "political action." Hence the S.P. will sacrifice anything for votes, relying on the ignis fatuus *of what its politicians, elected in such a way, will do in parliament. The S.L.P., on the contrary, sacrifices nothing for votes, knowing that the essential part of "political action" consists in the propaganda carried on at campaigns.*

—DANIEL DE LEON.

We shall either have Socialism—and that means that the State shall have vanished, or we shall preserve the State, and then we shall have no Socialism.

*

Capitalism is not to be saved. If Socialism does not triumph now, then imperialism will seize upon our society and establish a sort of feudo-capitalism that will set back the wheels of progress, and force freedom to start all over again along some fresh path.

—*DANIEL DE LEON.*

Index